The Newcomer Fieldbook

A Workbook Companion to *The Newcomer Student*

LOUISE EL YAAFOURI

Copyright © 2017 Louise El Yaafouri, Sidon Press

All rights reserved.

Library of Congress Control Number: 2017916545

ISBN 10: 099955428X

ISBN-13: 978-0-9995542-8-9

DEDICATION

This book is dedicated to the refugees and displaced people of the world. Your stories are often untold and your contributions immensely understated.   Let me be part of the chorus of voices that sings out,
You are human, you are seen and you are relevant.
It is my bold hope that humans can come together to recognize that the plight of one is the plight of us all; and the empowerment of one is the empowerment of us all.

And in memory of Michelle Buchi.   Your tremendous contributions to the world of education continue to ripple out into the world in the hearts and minds of our students. The joy, wisdom and laughter that you shared with your friends and loved ones has changed the course of many lives, including mine.

CONTENTS

Acknowledgments	i
Preface	iii
Acronym Legend	v
Introduction	1

1	Defining a Newcomer Program Vision	3
2	Program Audit & Goal Setting	9
3	Opening Doors: Intake Protocol	31
4	The Orientation Process	49
5	Diagnostic & Placement Testing	65
6	Progress Monitoring, Accommodations & Program Exit	77
7	Family Resource & Welcome Centers	101
8	Working Through Culture & Bias	111
9	Significant Stress & Trauma: Identification & Mitigation	127
10	Impactful Instructional Moves	147
11	Learning from the Experts:	177

The Voices of Exited Newcomer ELLs

ACKNOWLEDGMENTS

The writing of this book, like all seemingly impossible aims I am drawn to, is both for and because of my family. Cathryn Louise Acree, you continue to be my pillar in this world, and the best parts of me are rooted in you. To my parents- you gave me the gift of lessons of your own pasts, and then allowed me the room to explore the continents with all of my senses. Your support is the provenance of my courage. David and Danielle, only you have known the span of my life in full. Your energy is embedded in all that I do and in each word on these pages. To my newer, yet profoundly instrumental family- Zahi Yaafouri, Rajaa Dada, Samer Yaafouri and extended relatives. A vast ocean of cultural richness and human kindness is contained in the Yaafouri-Dada lineage- I aspire to maintain these traditions. You have made room for me in your world, and you've made it impossible for Lebanon to escape my heart.

Richard & Sue Kreuzer, your time, patience and guidance in editing this text are so very much appreciated. However, it is the kindness and gentleness that shines through you both that is most remarkable. You are treasures to many, myself included. My fellow teachers- Dr. Margaret Rohan, Judith Damas, Sabira Marike and so many others- you are my sounding boards, guides and greatest sources of inspiration. From the perspective of a teacher, the institution of education can be something of a carnival ride- full of unexpected twists and jolts. I wouldn't have survived the ride without you.

To Hani, I never saw you coming. You fill up the space of husband in ways that I never imagined as possibilities. Your inherent pull toward integrity and authenticity is unmatched. I strive to align my less-reliable compass to yours, for your path is inevitably one of kindness, honesty, optimism and a healthy outpouring of laughter. You've encouraged me beyond my known universe and past my threshold of comfort. Thank you for believing in me, even as I grow in learning to believe in myself. *Habibi ya elbi*- you are my everything.

To my students and the learners of the world, you are my purpose.

You- whatever your gender, skin color, religion, heritage, sexual orientation, natural abilities or opportunities for growth- go out and shine with all your strength. Do not shy away from your right and facility and responsibility to learn. You are capable of tremendous things and I am so very proud of you.

PREFACE

Throughout this discourse and for the purpose of maintaining consistency, a refugee person shall be noted according to the UNHCR 1951 Geneva Convention as one whom, "owing to a well-founded fear of being persecuted for reasons of race, religion, nationality, membership of a particular social group or political opinion, is outside the country of his nationality, and is unable to, or owing to such fear, is unwilling to avail himself of the protection of that country."

Additionally, the term "Newcomer" student will be defined as: a) any learner whose presence in the host country amounts to one year or less; b) any learner who is, or will be, receiving educational services in a language other than their native tongue; and c) any learner who does not demonstrate English language proficiency as indicated by state or district approved assessment instrument (i.e., WIDA ACCESS score of 5 or below).

For the purpose of clarity, please note that certain acronyms, which are common to the domain of English language acquisition, may be used throughout this text. A reminder index of acronyms can be found on the following page.

Additionally, content is organized in the following way. Main topics appear in the following font and style: Main Topic. Subtopics appear as: SUBTOPIC. Reproducible items are worksheets stand apart as such: Reproducible & Worksheet Materials.

I am so glad you are here.

Common Acronyms Related to English Instruction

BE: Bilingual Education

BICS: Basic Interpersonal Communication Skills

BINL: Basis Inventory of Natural Language

BoE: Body of Evidence

BSM Bilingual Syntax Measure

CALP: Cognitive Academic Language Proficiency

CCSS: Common Core State Standards

CELLA: Comprehensive English Language Assessment

CLO: Content Language Objective

DBT: Dialectical Behavior Therapy

EFL: English a Foreign Language

ELA: English Language Acquisition (This is confusing- check with your district!)

ELA: English Language Arts (This is confusing- check with your district!)

ELA-E: English Language Acquisition- English

ELA-S: English Language Acquisition- Spanish

ELD: English Language Development

ELDA: English Language Development Assessment

ELL: English Language Learner

ELP: English Language Proficiency

ENL: English as a New Language

ESL: English as a Second Language

ESOL: English to Speakers of Other Languages

ESEA: Elementary and Secondary Education Act

ESSA: Every Student Succeeds Act

ETS: Educational Testing Service

FAP: Fluent Academic Proficiency

GLAD: Guided Language Acquisition Design

HLS: Heritage Language Survey

IDEA: Individuals with Disabilities Education Act

IEP: Individualized Education Program

IPT: IDEA Proficiency Test (Ballard & Tighe)

ITDE: Instructional Technology/Distance Education

LAS Links: Language Assessment Systems Links

LAS: Language Assessment Scales

L1: A student's heritage or native language

L2: The language being taught, if outside the heritage language

LEP: Limited English Proficiency

NC: Newcomer

NCELA: NationalClearinghouse for English Language Acquisition

NCLB: No Child Left Behind

NEP: Non-English Proficient

NNS: Non-Native Speaker

PARCC: Partnership for Assessment of Readiness for College and Careers

PBIS: Positive Behavioral Intervention and Supports

PD: Professional Development

PTSS: Post-Traumatic Stress Syndrome

RCA4T: Refugees Class Assistance for Teacher

READ Act: Reading to Ensure Academic Development Act

RTI: Response to Intervention

SAL: Site Assessment Liaison

SIOP: Sheltered Instruction Observation Protocol

SLIFE: Students with Limited/Interrupted Formal Education

STT: Student Talk Time

TESL/TESOL: Teachers of Speakers of Other Languages

TEFL: Teachers of English as a Foreign Language

TTT: Teacher Talk Time

UNHCR: United Nations High Commissioner for Refugees

W-APT: WIDA Access Placement Test

WIDA: (no longer an acronym) World-Class Exceptional Design and Assessment

INTRODUCTION

In picking up this book, you have made a conscious choice to learn and develop as a professional. Congratulations! We are all in a continuous phase of learning. None of us have it all figured out, and none of us is a "perfect" educator. The context of education is constantly changing. Our student base is in continual flux, as are the needs of the populations we teach. Technology is ever evolving, and pedagogy seems to cycle back to us again and again. And so, as educators, we can never run out of room for growth.

In exploring refugee and immigrant Newcomer education, this is a great place to start. Please note that this resource is intended for use in association with the core text, *The Newcomer Student: An Educator's Guide to Aid Transition*. The book you are holding is the "nuts-and-bolts" application piece to the general principals outlined in the *Newcomer Student*; its contents are designed to be photocopied, adjusted, amended, and put to work.

The goals of The Newcomer Fieldbook are broad based. Readers will:
- Develop an understanding of the refugee and immigration processes;
- Learn to recognize and respond to cultural differences in the classroom;
- Identify key symptoms of traumatic upset and gain tools to address these needs;
- Explore best practices in Newcomer instruction and language learning;
- And gain efficacy in engaging Newcomer parents at school.

MUTUAL UNDERSTANDINGS

First, let's clarify a few critical components that carry over from the parent text. In the effort to resettle refugee populations into host societies, healthy integration is always the primary goal. Integration is the marker of holistic relocation and indicates full assimilation into the host culture without loss of heritage identity. When complete integration occurs, self-efficacy, self-worth, productivity and alacrity toward the host nation and its citizens are natural outcomes. Robust integration is critical. Often, this process begins in the classroom.

Newcomer students are identified as those learners who have been in the host country for one year or less and who are receiving education in a language that is outside of their heritage tongue. Many Newcomers have experienced a lapse in formal education. However, Newcomers also have a tremendous capacity for resilience, learning and socio-economic contribution. It is our responsibility to provide refugee Newcomer students with the tools and resources necessary to enable success in the host setting.

The refugee dynamic continues to influence the social and academic landscape of host nations. In the current era, we are seeing changes in the refugee-resettlement landscape that are unprecedented. It is in our cumulative best interest to be prepared to meet the demands of existing and incoming Newcomer populations with awareness, practicality and unified resolve.

FOUNDATIONS OF A SUCCESSFUL NEWCOMER PROGRAM

In the most ideal contexts, our schools and other educational organizations are preemptively prepared to meet the advanced needs and demands of Newcomer learners. Of course, the nature of world affairs is rarely within the realm of utter predictability. In these instances, we find ourselves constructing reactionary educational protocol for refugee Newcomer students. We are likely to discover that our traditional instructional systems are insufficient bolsters for refugee school success. For these students, proactive Newcomer ESL initiatives are a requisite for short and long-term socio-academic gain.

Newcomer programming must account for the complex emotional, psychological and learning needs of its participants. It must account for parent and family inclusion, cultural orientation, and language learning. In many instances, school-based Newcomer efforts must also incorporate registration assistance, translation services, health and immunization aid, and basic needs provisions. These programs are site-specific and are contingent upon the demographics of a school or community population. In short, there are no one-size-fits-all regimens.

However, generalized blueprints *can* be applied, and do provide a suitable launch point for initiation. The purpose of this text is to provide a map for the application of Newcomer-ESL education principles. The concepts are malleable by design and must be manipulated to suit the precise goals of its operational body.

Each objective is essential to overall program success. It is important to note that not all points or objectives can be achieved simultaneously. Effective Newcomer programs often require three to five years to realize a majority of intended outcomes.

Newcomer programming is a process, requiring persistent modulation and regulation. In the interest of time, it is necessary to limit the scope of discourse. First, the criticality of Newcomer parent involvement will be briefly addressed, supervened by discourse on effective Newcomer classroom instruction, as indicated by Objective 4. Thus, the primary foci will include: culture and diversity awareness training; learning implications of trauma and shock; and sheltered instruction techniques for educators.

Thank you for serving our students in your own unique capacity. Let's get to it!

1 DEFINING A NEWCOMER PROGRAM VISION

> **Guiding Questions for Chapter 1:**
> -- How do we, as a team, envision our optimal Newcomer-ESL program to look like?
> -- Can we best encapsulate these ideas into a mission and vision that will guide us in this process?
> -- What steps can we take immediately that will help us reach those aims?
> -- What steps can we project that will have long term, positive implications for our program?

Crafting a Successful Newcomer Program

You and your school are ready to grow in your capacity to serve the socio-academic needs of refugee and immigrant students, while expanding current learning opportunities for your "traditional" scholars. Great! So, where do we begin?

The answer is, we begin where *you* begin. You- *your* school or organization- will begin this journey at a unique map point. You may model yourselves after other successful programs; and later programs may follow your lead. But, your school cannot walk step-in-step with another Newcomer-ESL education initiative.

Why? Your school is not the same as any other school. Your specific student demographics are unmatched.

Your team of educators- their personalities, strengths, opportunities for growth- are exclusive to your campus. Your team's vision and goals and daily protocol are your own. Your children- the ones who stop to hug you on the way to the office, the ones you call out by first name for moving too quickly down the hallway, the ones you visit with in their homes on the weekends- these are *your* kids.

Who knows your students and their needs best? You do. Who knows the capacities and limitations of your space, resources and funding? You guessed it.

The word *crafting* in the section header is intentional. Your task is to craft- that is, to design and refine- a successful Newcomer-ESL program that works for your organization, based on your specific vision, goals, needs and available resources.

This workbook is designed to serve as a blueprint, not the Holy Grail. Just as in the parent text, *The Newcomer Student*, I invite you to manipulate, adjust, implement or even dismiss the individual resources you'll find in this book. Use what is meaningful and relevant to you, based on your organization's starting point.

Which leads us back to our question. *Where do we begin?*

DEFINING MISSION AND VISION STATEMENTS

Mission and vision statements are cornerstones in determining your group's purpose and function. These declarations help to ground and guide your team as a unified organism with a clearly defined cause. Mission and vision statements are more than formalities.

Once they are established, they also serve as a baseline rubric for evaluating all decisions and outcomes. Your team can ask, "Does this item align with our mission and vision? If not, how can we effectively adjust or release it?"

Your mission statement defines what your group aims to accomplish in the present context- *right now*. The goals outlined in the mission declaration should be realistic and attainable. The vision statement outlines your team's long-term objectives or ideals- your vision for the future.

Let's look at some broad examples. Here's Google's mission statement: "Google's mission is to organize the world's information and make it universally accessible and useful". Their vision statement is "to organize all of the data in the world and make it accessible for everyone in a useful way". (Google online, 2016)

Google works to organize and make information accessible *right now*. Organizing data for the entire world is a lofty objective that will take time, but could actually be accomplished at some point in the future.

Mission and vision declarations do not need to be complicated. In fact, simplicity is best. Ikea's current mission is to "*make everyday life better* for their customers". *Current* is emphasized because mission statements can be utterly static and should be revisited frequently as the team's success or understanding progresses.

Meanwhile, Ikea's vision is, "to create a better everyday life for many people. We make this possible by offering a wide range of well-designed, functional home-furnishing products at prices so low that as many people as possible will be able to afford them." The phrasing *as many people as possible* indicates a long-range goal, or vision, for the future.

I bet you're thinking, "That's great, but why are we talking about Fortune 500 companies? We're trying to get our Newcomer Centers and ELL programming off the ground!" Well, we can approach that very aim from a business minded perspective. In this context, mission and vision statements are certainly applicable. Let's examine some approaches in the educational realm.

Pearson Education details their vision and mission as:

"Our Vision: To fulfill the educational needs across a spectrum of individuals with reliable experience and technology. Our Mission:

- *To provide end-to-end education solutions in the K-12 segment.*
- *To become a leader in the education services field.*
- *To create comprehensive educational content that can be delivered through a series of innovative mechanisms, thus removing physical and cultural barriers in knowledge dissemination.*
- *To be a vehicle of change by creating interfaces that allow education to reach the underprivileged."* (Pearson online, 2016)

As we narrow our interest, here are a few inspiring examples specifically related to refugee and immigrant Newcomer educational services. Canada's Southwest Newcomer Welcome Centre services refugees and immigrants in multiple capacities. Their mission is, *"To enable independence and respectful community participation for Newcomers to Canada by providing settlement and integration services in a safe and welcoming environment, and by promoting cross cultural awareness to all in the communities we serve."*

Southwest Newcomer Centre's Vision is more objective. It calls for the center, *"To be a comprehensive newcomer service providing agency acting as a gateway to equitable, respectful, welcoming communities where all members are empowered to actively participate and contribute."*

Austin, Minnesota is a refugee hub with a thriving Newcomer Welcome Center. It also has a clear mission statement:

> *"The Welcome Center serves the City of Austin as the community's multi-cultural center, building community by welcoming newcomers, supporting residents in transition and creating access and opportunity."* Austin's vision holds that, *"The Welcome Center envisions a vibrant and culturally diverse community where everyone is accepted, respected and independent."*

HOW DO WE CREATE OUR OWN M/V STATEMENTS?

First, gather your team. Mission and vision objectives are not one-man (or woman) shows. Make room for ideas to circulate. Open the floor. Disagree. Break thinking down and re-configure it. Decide what's best for your team. Then, decide what's best for the population you serve and override the interests of the team. This is a time for finding your organization's core. All outward momentum will come from this center, so be sure it's solid. (Or at least, that it is stable enough to bear the weight and stress of the current and future objectives you will set for your organization).

Then, jump in. Here are a few guiding questions as you begin your thinking around mission and vision statements:

- *Who are we serving?*
- *What are the precise demographics of the population that we are serving?*
- *What do we want to accomplish?*
- *What do we aim to provide?*
- *By what means will we accomplish these aims?*
- *How will our efforts enable student success?*
- *Why is the student success we defined important?*
- *How will we measure/determine success?*
- *How will our efforts better our school and community?*

Next, elaborate on your values. What character traits, key ethics or primary goals does your organization consider sacred or essential to program success? How does or will your team maintain its integrity? Values encompass qualities such as leadership, partnership, innovation, safety, continuous growth and improvement, accountability, and professionalism. What does your team stand for?

Now, begin to work together to invent (or revisit) your statements. There is no right or wrong way or any blanket format. Find what works best. You can start big (vision) and bring those ideas into clear, applicable focus (mission). Or, flip the process and move outward toward your team's vision.

Come back to your M/V statements regularly. To reinforce their importance, begin and end meetings with them, especially in the beginning stages. Remind each other to check in with your team's core values throughout decision-making processes. Let your mission and vision define your team's work.

As a Newcomer-focused educational consultant, my professional objectives read:

*My **mission** is to empower educators to provide Newcomer ELLs and all students with the tools, resources and support they need to achieve their highest academic and social capacity.*

*My **vision** is that all learners have an equitable right to high quality education and upward social mobility. All learners possess an ability to achieve greatness. All educators have an equitable right to training and support that enhances student growth. All teachers are capable of instructional excellence.*

What is your team's mission and vision?

2 PROGRAM AUDIT & GOAL SETTING

> ### Guiding Questions for Chapter 2:
> -- How do we, as a team, define our program goals and objectives?
> -- What is our plan to break these goals and objectives into bite-sized, attainable pieces?
> -- As we work through this plan, what ideas, new implementation and/or protocol changes stand out?
> -- How will we choose to structure our ELL programming? Or, how can we make the most of/expand the systems we already have in place?
> -- Who are our available in-building and community resources that can contribute to the development and success of our program?

Newcomer-ESL Program Audit

Before I enter a school or organization for consulting purposes, I always ask the administrative team or program head to complete (or at least work through) what I refer to as a Newcomer Program Audit. It sounds a bit daunting, but I assure you, this is only a tool!

The audit can be very helpful in pointing out existing strengths as well as areas for development. For the person or team completing the survey, it serves to highlight areas of success and concern. Very often, it also brings to light areas that had never been considered before. This is my favorite part. This is the realm of possibility.

As a consultant, the Newcomer-ESL Program Audit is useful in determining a realistic starting point. Some organizations are in the earliest stages of development and planning, others are strategically sound and prepared for enhancing existing policies and practices. Neither situation is inherently stellar or less-than-stellar. They simply are, and both have room for growth. They are simply at different locations on the map.

Take a few moments (or a few days) to complete the survey. Give your responses the time and thought they deserve. Consult other decision makers and your most valuable resources (ahem, your teachers!) in the building. Think like a child- don't be afraid to say, "I don't know" and remain open to ideas and thoughts as they present themselves. Work toward discovering your starting point. Once you get there, just be still in that place for a week or two. Don't rush to make any quick adjustments. Observe your surroundings and school operations with a closer eye. Adjust your start point as necessary. Then, get ready to grow.

Newcomer Specialist Esther Mathoka, sharing her strategy with Dr. Margaret Rohan; visual learning and professional development at Isabella Bird Community School.

Newcomer-ESL Program Audit

Name of program: _____

Name of School: _____

Ages/Grades of school: _____

Ages/Grades involved in Newcomer programming: _____

Contact Person: _____

Role in Newcomer Programming: _____

Email: _____

Phone: _____

Secondary Contact Person: _____

Role in Newcomer Programming: _____

Email: _____

Phone: _____

Description of Program

Program's definition of "Newcomer":

_____

_____

_____

Program's specification for identifying eligible Newcomer students:

_____

_____

_____

Intended length of Newcomer programming:

_____

_____

Describe which period(s)/hour(s) of the day and/or what subject area(s) will eligible students participate in Newcomer-specific sheltered instruction courses:

_____

_____

Describe your school's distinction between Newcomer and ESL Level 1 placement:

_____

_____

Name determining factors for Newcomer placement:

_____

_____

_____

Name qualifying factors for Newcomer progress monitoring:

_____

_____

_____

Name qualifying factors for Newcomer program exit:

_____

_____

_____

Describe policies regarding distribution of earned credit for students who are enrolled in Newcomer programming.

_____

_____

_____

_____

Identify alternative ELA/ELD learning opportunities (including tutoring, summer school and Saturday school) for eligible Newcomer students:

_____

_____

_____

_____

_____

Description of Instructional Services

Describe your school's ideal Newcomer class size:

Minimum _____ Maximum _____

Identify type(s) of ongoing ELD support programming for exited Newcomer students:

_____

_____

_____

Identify curricula pieces that will apply to Newcomer specific learning:

Literacy:_____

Writing:_____

Speaking:_____

ESL/ELD:_____

Mathematics:_____

Science:_____

Health:_____

Social Studies:_____

Cultural Orientation:_____

Study Skills:_____

Other:_____

Describe expected instructional techniques to be implemented with fidelity in Newcomer ELD classrooms:

_____

_____

_____

Describe expected environmental factors to be present in Newcomer ELD classrooms:

_____
_____
_____

Description of Exemptions

Describe policy for standardized testing exemptions for identified Newcomers:

_____
_____
_____
_____

Describe policy for site-specific exemptions for identified Newcomers:

_____
_____
_____
_____

Describe policy for _____ exemptions for identified Newcomers:

_____
_____
_____
_____

Description of Educator Effectiveness Training

Describe the key qualities and strengths of an exemplary Newcomer teacher, according to the specific needs and vision of your school:

_____
_____
_____
_____

Identify essential and preferred prerequisites for potential Newcomer teachers:

ESSENTIAL   PREFERRED

_____   _____
_____   _____
_____   _____
_____   _____
_____   _____

What training initiatives are currently in place in the areas of:

TRAUMA/SHOCK _____

CULTURE/DIVERSITY _____

ELD INSTRUCTION _____

DATA TRACKING _____

PARENT COMMUNICATION _____

TECHNOLOGY _____

Describe gaps or opportunities in current PD structures related to Newcomers:

_____
_____
_____
_____

Name and describe **teacher evaluation** policies/rubrics in Newcomer classrooms:

_____
_____
_____
_____
_____

Name key support personnel for Newcomer teachers:

NAME	ROLE

Name key texts, websites and resources for Newcomer teachers:

_____
_____
_____
_____

Description of Mental Health Supports for Newcomers

Describe socio-emotional supports that are available to students at your school:

_____
_____
_____
_____

Name key **school-based** support personnel for Newcomer students:

NAME	ROLE
_____	_____
_____	_____
_____	_____
_____	_____

Name key **community-based** supports for Newcomer students and their families:

NAME	SERVICE
_____	_____
_____	_____
_____	_____
_____	_____

Description of Program Evaluation

Describe the policy for evaluating effectiveness of Newcomers program:

_____

_____

_____

_____

Identify data points and assessment measures to be included in program evaluation:

_____	_____
_____	_____
_____	_____
_____	_____
_____	_____

Frequency of program evaluations:

_____

_____

_____

Describe processes for initiating amendments to existing program:

_____

_____

_____

_____

_____

Identify thoughts and ideas that presented themselves during the audit process and/or apparent professional development needs and opportunities in the area of Newcomer intake, evaluation, monitoring and instruction:

_____
_____
_____
_____
_____
_____
_____
_____
_____

Using the Audit to Inform Growth:

NAMING AN ACTION PLAN, GOALS, & OBJECTIVES

The central purpose of the Newcomer-ESL Program Audit is to guide and inform positive forward momentum in relevant, meaningful ways. As a consultant, my job is to help clients evaluate their honest survey responses, and to draft a framework of actionable steps that lead to a desired set of school-specific outcomes.

This process is most enjoyable (and most effective) when it is conducted in a participative group setting, in which the consultant simply acts as a facilitator. Buy-in for "prescription" services is almost always limited. Therefore, I encourage as much staff feedback and interaction as possible in creating viable next-steps. If you are charged with evaluating the survey results for your organization, my advice is: don't go it alone. Rally the troops and get the entire team on board. Do this in the earliest possible decision making phases. This effort fosters essential investment from all staff- your most prized stakeholders.

The following is a very typical example of a Newcomer-ESL Program "Action Plan". This particular version was the outcome of a goal-setting workshop for a Denver- based high school. The school's Newcomer Center was in its infancy when these objectives were created. Accordingly, their agenda reflects foundational needs and requirements and is unique to their own population and school culture.

In this scenario, we fleshed out each of the school's Top Five, indicated as (A)- (E). After this, we crafted objective statements. In this context, we wrote four, not five objectives. Finally, we elaborated on specific success demonstrators, or sub-goals, for each objective.

Feel free to utilize this example as a template in creating your own version. Highlight those places you might have starred, circled or underlined while completing the audit, and make those areas focal points.

Do avoid tackling too much at once. Creating, organizing, managing and improving Newcomer programming is an enormous feat. It is doable, but not overnight. Give your team room to expand organically. Treat the process like a marathon- slow down and pace yourself. Set small, measureable goals. Then, break those goals down into even more manageable steps. Take time to acknowledge and reflect on achievements met along the way!

SAMPLE ACTION PLAN

Through careful design and responsive allocation, _____ School will ensure Newcomer ELL school success in the following capacities:

A) Values in Newcomers making progress toward English mastery can only be fully attained when the district and participating schools have created a clear vision and plan for services to be rendered, processes of evaluation and expected outcomes.

To address these specific aims, we will work directly with key personnel to accomplish and/or clarify the following:

1. Explicitly identify Academic Goals for Newcomer ELLs
2. Develop a Mission and Vision Statement
3. Organize and Manage Newcomer Family Welcome Center
4. Establish and structure Newcomer-specific teams and team leads
5. Map out student and parent orientation efforts
a. Evaluate specific needs of target populations
b. Build parent and community outreach efforts
c. Train staff in understanding Culture & Diversity
d. Train staff in understanding Trauma, Loss & Shock
6. Determine logistical issues
7. Develop and organize in-building resources
8. Develop and organize out-of-building and community resources

B) Number and percentage of students attaining English will increase in direct relation and proportion to items evidenced in (A). With regard to Newcomer ELL transition, our firm will provide forms and protocol for these procedures (including Newcomer Transition Markers form and Newcomer Academic Markers form), and will effectively prepare program organizers to implement them across a network of applicable schools and service providers. Explicit timelines for submission of materials will be determined at the start of service.

C) Student participation will be increased via processes of accurate incoming placement. Through the Welcome Center, parents will be made aware of specific opportunities that enhance learner achievement, such as Newcomer ELL-focused tutoring, online, class enrollment options and available language-based assessment accommodations.

In an operative capacity, teachers and staff will receive consistent and ongoing training and coaching in Newcomer ELL instruction. Professional development will encompass: individual biases workshops, culture and diversity training, sheltered instruction techniques, and best practices in Newcomer ELL education. The tools and strategies shared in our trainings have a demonstrated success, equating to multiple years' growth in single school years for non-English speaking students.

D) As students develop proficiency in social and conversational English, they will also realize pronounced gains across content areas. Additionally, staff will be trained to create and refer to CLOs in all subject areas. Thus, content language learning will become an embedded facet throughout the school day. Finally, educators will be coached in planning for and providing multiple ways for students to access content understanding and demonstrate proficiency in a content area, even with limited English capacity. These sheltered instruction practices will incorporate graphic organizers, co-operative structures, and hands-on demonstration outlets.

E) Yearly progress of ELs will be measured according to existing assessment frameworks. Additionally, students will be monitored via WIDA ACCESS and/or WAPT testing frameworks. Additionally, Newcomer ELL progress will be monitored throughout the school year according to: classroom assessment and data collection (body of evidence); documented movement along Newcomer advancement/mobility rubric; and documented activity in teacher accountability process, along defined rubric.

STATED GOALS & OBJECTIVE STATEMENTS

As a team, you've thought through your Action Plan. Now, it's important to section larger items into pieces that can be conceptualized and processed. In our teaching, we deconstruct whole concepts, themes or units into digestible bits for our students. We spread out related lessons over a period of days or weeks. We don't expect our students to demonstrate immediate proficiency in an area.

We can allow ourselves the same space to learn and achieve in attainable steps.

Working from the Action Plan, the next step is to determine overarching goals. From our goals, we will derive our objectives. For our purposes, it is important to differentiate between *goals* and *objectives*. Essentially, goals represent the big-picture view; objectives hold the fine print. My favorite clarification of this idea, from Tulane University:

"A **goal** is an overarching principle that guides decision making.

Objectives are specific, measurable steps that can be taken to meet the **goal**."

Returning to the sample NC high school Action Plan, our next step was to create appropriate goal and objective statements. The number of goals a school will have can vary. They can be long-term goals, or divided by units of time, as indicated here.

_____ School Recommended Period 1 Goals

Goal Statement 1: _____ *will directly endorse overall Newcomer social-academic success through the establishment of a school-based Newcomer welcome center, which will function as a centralized location for Newcomer enrollment assistance, orientation programming, family resources accessibility (including language services) and community engagement.*

Objectives for Period (1):

- _____ will announce a mission and vision for its Newcomer programming, including the Welcome Center
- Newcomer Welcome center will be fully accessible to families, with resources available to clients in physical and on-line capacities.
- Direct face-to-face contact has been made with 100% of eligible families in the first year.
- Participation rates for participating families will grow by 70% the first year, as determined by attendance logs, exit tickets and liaison reports.
- > 80% or more of the parents and students who take a baseline assessment for host cultural nuances will increase their score by 1 or more number value points (on a scale of 1-5) within the first academic year.
- _____ will begin to develop a complete manual of resources, parent forms, Newcomer placement and evaluation protocol, and community agencies related to Newcomer populations.

Goal Statement 2: _____ *will establish and maintain efficient record keeping systems for the purposes of registering, monitoring, assessing and graduating Newcomer learners.*

Objectives for Period (1):

- 100% of families who are enrolled in programming will be accurately identified as eligible for services.
- 100% of individuals and/or families serviced have accurately maintained records that can be readily accessed at any time.

Goal Statement 3: _____ *will establish and maintain efficient communication systems with Newcomer parents and students and will make evident student eligibility for any and all programs related to language learning and/or socio-academic success.*

Objectives for Period (1):

- 100% of Newcomer family phone numbers will be verified for accuracy in the first year.
- The Welcome Center will house language translation services. Where specific language services are not available, Welcome Center will provide multiple-language "top forms" that describe the need to have items translated.
- The Welcome Center will prepare itself to become a center for adult resources, including adult ESL programming and school orientation.
- 100% of families who are identified as Newcomers will be enrolled in one or more additional services for which they are eligible, including tutoring, "buddy" programs, or computerized language-learning services.

_____ School Recommended Period 2 Goals

Goal Statement 1: _____ *will empower teachers to give Newcomer-ELL students the tools and support they need to achieve academic and social success.*

Objectives for Period (2):

- **Teachers and staff will engage in a series of professional development opportunities that address:**
  - Program mission/vision, goals, and processes
  - Refugee/immigrant intake processes
  - Biases exploration
  - Culture and Diversity sensitivity training
  - Trauma and shock
  - Newcomer best practices, including sheltered instruction techniques and SIOP planning.
- Teachers and school staff who are surveyed ahead of Cultural and Diversity Sensitivity Training will demonstrate an average score increase of 50% or more from pre-survey to post-survey.
- Teachers and school staff who are surveyed ahead of Sheltered Instruction for ELLs Training will demonstrate an average score increase of 50% or more from pre-survey to post-survey.
- Teachers and school staff who are observed before training and feedback sessions will demonstrate an average score increase of 50% or greater in the final observation, according to the District Evaluation Rubric for Newcomer Instruction.
- Eligible Newcomer ELL students will demonstrate reading and math gains of 1.5 years growth or higher in a single academic school year.
- > 70% of eligible students enroll in tutoring or other available EL programming in the first academic year

Clarifying Your Program Framework

ELL programming is not a homogeneous application. In fact, there are many different channels to achieve the aim of targeted, accelerated academic language instruction. It will be up to you and your key stakeholders to determine the mode or combination of modes that will best service your specific student population, school culture and available resources.

"Newcomer" initiatives are unique in that they are designated as such according to units of time. Newcomer programming, in principle, is designed to occur for two full semesters, at which point participating students transition into traditional mainstream coursework for the duration of their school career (though they may still be eligible to receive supplementary English support services).

However, certain exceptions are made. If, after two semesters, a student is not making the appropriate academic progress toward exit criteria, and if such evidence suggests that such gap would significantly impair a child's opportunity to fully participate and succeed in a mainstream learning environment, he or she may be referred for additional Newcomer services.

Newcomer policy differs from General ELA-E services (such as ESL for Spanish speakers or ESL pull-out sessions for mainstreamed Newcomers), which are not time contingent. The latter are based wholly on host language skill and ability level, such that as long as a student evidences a need for language-building capacity, he or she will remain eligible for these services.

Let's take a look at the most common language service programs. Be thinking about which services already exist on your campus or which specific styles (or combinations) might be the best fit for your campus.

PROGRAM MODELS FOR LANGUAGE LEARNING

Dual Language: Learners are instructed in and encouraged to interact in both the heritage and the host language, **with a goal of developing and maintaining proficiency in both.** ELA-S (Spanish) programs are the most prevalent form of dual language education in the U.S.

_____   _____

NUMBER OF D/L STUDENTS   PERCENTAGE OF D/L STUDENTS

Transitional Bilingual: Learners are *initially* instructed in and encouraged to interact both the heritage and host languages, **with a goal of developing English proficiency and fully transitioning to mainstream programming.** In this way, the heritage language is slowly phased out as English language abilities increase.

_____   _____

NUMBER OF T/B STUDENTS   PERCENTAGE OF T/B STUDENTS

Newcomer Programming: Using Sheltered Instruction techniques and a range of socio-linguistic supports, learners are instructed in and encouraged to interact in English, **with a goal of developing English proficiency and fully transitioning to mainstream programming.** Newcomer instruction may encompass other areas, including Western norms and values; trauma and shock mitigation; health and wellness protocol and additional parent-outreach efforts.

_____   _____

NUMBER OF N/C STUDENTS   PERCENTAGE OF N/C STUDENTS

Tier 2 ELL/ESL Services: Tier 2 Services enable eligible students to participate in Push-In/Pull-Out resources for English language development, **with a goal of enhancing English language abilities after a child has been mainstreamed.** In Push-In settings, a language specialist will meet and work with the child in his or her classroom, while Pull-Out options call for students to leave the homeroom for established durations to work on language development in individual or small group contexts. Programs will vary by school design.

_____   _____

NUMBER OF TIER 2 STUDENTS   PERCENTAGE OF TIER 2 STUDENTS

Sample Mission, Vision and Goals Package:
ISABELLA BIRD COMMUNITY SCHOOL, DENVER, CO

We'll finish this chapter by looking at an end result. I use the term *end result* loosely, because schools are static places, and programs need to have some built-in flexibility such that they adapt to changes in student demographics, leadership and other variables. When all of this digging and brainstorming turns into action, you will have a true vision and direction for your Newcomer program. We'll return to "Izzy B" as our example.

Isabella Bird Community School is a refugee-Newcomer magnet school located in Denver, Colorado. The demographic of the school is unique in that the larger student body is comprised of mostly affluent, American-born neighborhood students. At the time this document was created, IBCS was also home to nearly eighty refugee or immigrant Newcomer ELLs.

This document was created by the leadership team at Isabella Bird as part of the consulting/coaching process. It is a great example and template for clear, purposeful direction in program direction and organization.

Our mission and purpose for the IBCS Newcomer Program is as follows:

Mission: The goal of the IBCS newcomer program is to accelerate language learning to support content instruction, and to help students adapt to American school culture in a nurturing and supportive learning environment.

Purpose: The purpose of the newcomer program is to provide students with a foundation of language, content and cultural instruction before transitioning them into traditional mainstream programming.

Our school-wide values:

I will act in ways that are safe for everyone. I will treat myself, others, and our environment with care. I will do my best learning and help others to do their best learning.

Isabella Bird Community School: Newcomer Program Audience

- The IBCS Newcomer program is designed for Early Childhood Education (ECE)-5th grade students who have limited or interrupted formal education and who have not yet attained host language fluency.
- Newcomer students will transition to the mainstream classroom when they meet exit criteria or after two semesters in a Newcomer classroom. Exceptions may occur if and when a student is referred to the Instructional Services Advisory (ISA) team for consideration of extended services, and if the body of evidence is sufficient to support such a decision.
- Newcomer students will engage with native English-speaking peers during recess, lunch, field trips and "SAMPLES" periods (physical education, music, technology, art). Additional opportunities for ELL and non-ELL student interaction will include afterschool programming, reading pals and Newcomer buddies.
- Parents have a legal right to refuse Newcomer classroom placement and/or targeted English Language services on behalf of their child.

Isabella Bird Community School: Newcomer Program Goals

- Our instruction is asset based and tailored to our students' individual needs.
- All cultures represented at IBCS are valued.
- The school community makes school-wide decisions through a culturally sensitive lens.
- Educational experiences and field trips are important experiences intended to build background knowledge and vocabulary. All students have the opportunity to participate in such experiences without financial limitation.
- Newcomer students will be assigned a buddy and given an orientation tour.
- Neighborhood students and Newcomer students will work together to develop their multicultural understanding and promote intercultural communication.
- All students are invited to take risks and all students have access to scaffolded content.
- When students leave the Newcomer program, they will be able to perform successfully in a traditional mainstream classroom.

IBCS: Newcomer Program Features

- The Newcomer program is distinct from regular ESL
- Scaffolded instruction strategies, including Guided Language Acquisition Design (GLAD) techniques and co-operative talk structures are implemented in all classrooms across all content areas to integrate language and content learning.
- Newcomer classrooms provide an orientation to U.S. schools and culture for students and their families.
- Newcomer students are exposed to appropriate grade level content learning and are held to high academic expectations.
- Curricula selection and instructional techniques support students at all language-learning levels, including those with no/low literacy and/or limited formal schooling.
- IBCS teachers are experienced in and passionate about working with Newcomer populations.

- IBCS teachers take part in regular professional development related to best practices in Newcomer instruction.
- Leadership organizes relevant, quality professional development opportunities; holds all teachers to high standards; and communicates expectations to teachers. Leadership is directly responsible for providing consistent, ongoing support and feedback to all staff with the aim of enhancing teacher efficacy and positively impacting student gain.
- Family connections are built through home visits, Newcomer family meetings and school-hosted events.
- We are thorough and purposeful in our staffing and assignment processes, taking into account the specific needs of the IBCS student body and the vision for our school.

IBCS: Statement of Language Learning Aims

At Isabella Bird Community School, we recognize that language learning opens doors to new cultures, perspectives, understandings and opportunities.

Each of our students is a new language learner.

Our traditional English speakers are also Spanish language learners. In addition to their heritage language capacities, our Newcomers are also ELLs.

We recognize that each of our students is highly capable of heritage and host language fluency, and that language instruction is embedded in all facets, in all subjects and in every area of the school, throughout each school day.

We believe that fostering language acquisition is a whole-school responsibility.

We are committed to helping our students achieve language success. Our goals in this regard are that:

- All classes and content areas are opportunities to learn and practice English in a safe, supportive environment.
- All students are held to high learning expectations.
- Each school day is crafted to promote language learning in meaningful contexts.
- All students engage in sustained interactions with teachers and peers, are presented with ongoing opportunities to interact in ways that support the construction of knowledge.
- All teachers are masterful in devising and sharing purposeful, comprehensive Content Language Objectives (CLOs).
- All teachers are masterful in making content language accessible through scaffolded instruction techniques.
- All teachers are masterful in promoting deep disciplinary discovery and generative cognitive processing.
- Leadership has a strong presence in our building and supports teachers through feedback, mentorship and the provision of quality, ongoing opportunities for professional growth and learning.
- All IBCS staff and leadership are masterful in using data to drive instruction for all students, including ELLs.

3 OPENING DOORS: INTAKE PROTOCOL

> **Guiding Questions for Chapter 3:**
> -- What district, state and national requirements for student enrollment must we be informed about?
> -- How do we, as a team, clarify our intake procedures?
> -- Where and how do we store blank intake documents?
> -- Who are these documents available to?
> -- Where and how do we store and secure completed documents?
> -- How will we use intake data to inform our decisions and protocol?
> -- Who/what team at our location will be held accountable for ensuring the validity and consistency of student intake procedures?

Chapter 2 focused on getting your team fitted with essential organizational resources and tools that can be made-to-measure and implemented *right now*. Here, we'll begin by looking at student intake and home data collection.

We'll move through this section quickly. Every district and school has its own general enrollment process. I will briefly speak to enrollment criteria and protocol that is relevant to ELL student processing.

First and foremost, it is always important to remember (and to inform parents) that *school enrollment information can never be used to call into question the legal status of a child, parent or family member.* Registration data and accompanying documentation can be used for the singular purpose of student registration. Parents who wish to register their child in a U.S. public school must provide proof in three domains: residency, age, and social security. To clarify, the U.S. Department of Justice and the U.S. Department of Education provide that,

> "All children in the United States are entitled to equal access to a basic public elementary and secondary education regardless of their actual or perceived race, color, national origin, citizenship, immigration status, or the status of their parents/guardians. School districts that either prohibit or discourage, or maintain policies that have the effect of prohibiting or discouraging, children from

enrolling in schools because they or their parents/guardians are not U.S. citizens or are undocumented may be in violation of Federal law."

Essential Applications: Enrollment

Well, here we are. If I guessed correctly, you're here too, and very likely did not read the pages leading up to this one. I know, I get it. We're educators. We're strapped for time. We want to just get in there and get things done! We needed practical applications, like, yesterday. Am I right?

If so, I will kindly ask you to set the book down gently, take a few deep breaths, and rewind to Chapter 1. Like any great undertaking, our effort to create, grow or refine a Newcomer program deserves a solid foundation. This does not have to be an instantaneous construction process. A few extra days or weeks of careful planning will not drastically harm our schools or students. Rushed, frantic, unorganized decision-making will.

If you've been following along with us, good news. Welcome to the first "Applications" section. These sections will be your go-to areas of the book if you are looking for key forms, templates and examples.

If the shoe fits… great! Leave the template you are aiming for as is and put it into practice. If you see loops and holes and ways to make it better for you and your team, even better!

THE ELL-SPECIFIC REGISTRATION PROCESS

In the overwhelming majority of public school districts, the protocol for registering ELLs is as follows. Of course, always check for compliance and alignment.

1. At the time of registration, parents will be asked to complete a Heritage Language Survey- also called a Home Language Survey (HLS) or Home Language Questionnaire (HLQ). Most school districts offer a standardized HLS form.
2. The HLS asks a series of questions related to the student's native language, the language(s) spoken in the home, and the level of exposure to English. If the HLS indicates that the child may be an English Language Learner (ELL), he or she may be referred for language testing in order to determine eligibility for targeted ELD programming.
3. Students who are referred for language ability testing may be evaluated using school/district placement assessments, most commonly W-APT or WIDA.
4. If and when such assessments indicate ELD eligibility, the student will be recommended for class placement that is inclusive of these services. The parents will be invited to approve, in writing, the decision to enroll students in ELD-specific programming. Of course, parents do have a legal right to refuse these services, although this very rarely occurs.
5. The student is actively enrolled in Newcomer programming or ELD pull-out and/or push-in services.

With regard to registering Newcomer-ESL students, it is helpful to have as much additional information about the student and his or her family as possible. Such processes can be quite simplistic, or detailed and extensive. Again, the type of language survey(s) used should reflect the needs of the school and its population. I like to aim for somewhere in the middle, aiming for an understanding, without overwhelming. We'll get to some examples in just a moment.

CREATING A SYSTEM

Student intake, even that pertaining to ELLs, should not be rocket science. However, it is critical to develop systems for this process. Clarity and consistency create calm. They are also essential in covering both legal and organizational ground.

Intake protocol will vary by district, and sometimes by school, too. Your procedures should make sense for your organization. It is also imperative that they take into careful account national, state and district expectations for student enrollment, registration and ELL placement.

Each time I work with schools in creating these documents, we begin by examining current intake procedures. Here are some of the questions I asked in that process: Who are the first school personnel that potential students and their family members see when they walk in the door? Exactly how is registration handled? What about secondary processes for probable ELLs? How consistent are these procedures? Who is aware that they exist? Where is registration information stored? Who checks files for accuracy?

Asking questions and evaluating responses alongside school administrators always reveals a few surprises- and a lot of loopholes. In this space, we have room and perspective to analyze what works and what doesn't, what to keep and what to toss. We are also able to determine critical missing links (communication and clarity usually take the top spots), and get to work filling those holes in purposeful, directed ways. Again, the focus is simplicity.

As we worked through this very process at Isabella Bird, we were cognizant of specific site-based needs, including staffing concerns, time and other available (and unavailable) resources. We also kept a close eye to district mandates (Isabella Bird adheres to an established district Heritage Language Survey, for example), as well as state and federal laws, especially those around equitable access to education and official record keeping).

Below are two documents (merged onto one page) that came out of those sessions. You will notice that they are clean and clear. The fluff has been omitted. We are not creating college thesis papers; we are creating systems that any person, at any time, can easily read and act on. One of my favorite quotes in this regard comes from esteemed engineer and statistician, W. Edwards Deming: *"If you can't describe what you are doing as a process, you don't know what you are doing."*

IBCS Student Intake Procedure

1. Welcome: All parents, students and community members are greeted in a warm, timely manner.

2. Prospective families will complete registration paperwork and provide all necessary legal documentation.

3. Parents will complete a heritage language survey on behalf of registering student.

4. Students who demonstrate probable eligibility for ELA services according to the Heritage Language Survey (HLS) are tested for language placement.

5. Class registration is processed, based on evaluation of placement data and/or alternative placement evidence.

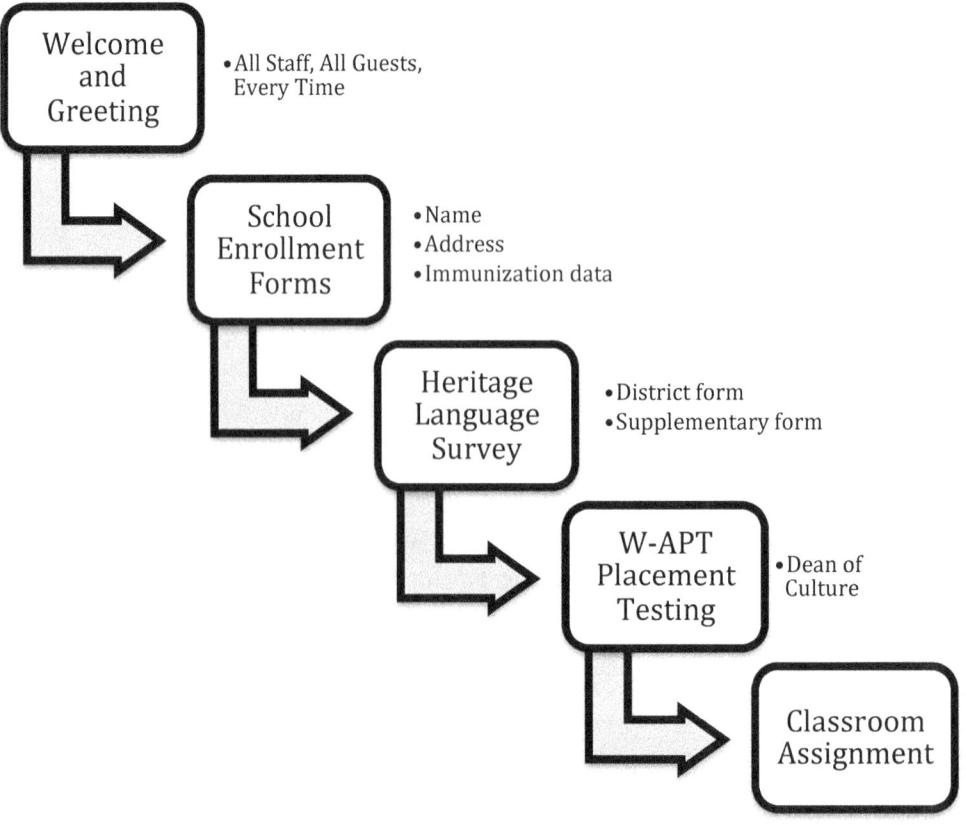

Notice of Language Services Eligibility

The _____ School District offers English Language Development programming to students who are new to the English language or have not developed full proficiency in the English language.

English Language Development (ELD) services are free for qualified students. ELD access is a right for all students whose primary (home) language is not English.

Your child, _____ has been recommended to participate in English Language Development (ELD) services at _____school.

The purpose of ELD programming is to ensure English language proficiency for non-English speakers. The program explicitly teaches students listening, speaking, reading and writing skills. Specialized ELD instruction facilitates access to grade-level content at all language-learning levels. ELD programming helps English Learners positively transition to general education classrooms. As parents, you have the right to:

- Receive timely notice of all eligible opportunities for your child to succeed at school, including English language services, tutoring, testing exemptions and specialized learning programs.
- Conference with your child's teacher and/or school administrators to discuss your child's school progress and program exit
- Visit ELD classes and services that your child attends
- Withdraw your child from ELD services

Unless otherwise notified, your child will be enrolled in ELD programming, effective _____/_____/_____.

If you choose to refuse or withdraw your child from ELD services, please complete ELD Program Refusal form and return it to the school office or your child's teacher. I have read and understand this statement and/or this statement has been read or translated for me, and I understand its contents.

Name _____Signature_____

Date _____Translator_____

Heritage Language Surveys

Heritage Language Surveys (also called Home Language Surveys or Home Language Questionnaires) are used in the initial process of identifying students who may be eligible to receive ELL services. A heritage language survey usually takes the form of a brief questionnaire, which may be administered in English print, native language print, orally, or through a translator. The purpose of the survey is to establish an understanding of a student's language-learning background.

HLS responses may indicate a child's initial eligibility for ELL services. Here's an example: Khaled's family has just arrived to register him for school. The family meets with an enrollment specialist at the school. When completing the survey, Khaled's mother indicates that they are from Somalia. She also notes that Somali is the language spoken in the home. However, Khaled's first language (and only instructional language) is Swahili, as the family relocated to the refugee camp in Kenya just before Khaled's birth. Khaled's exposure to the English language, at least according to the Heritage Language Survey, is very limited.

Khaled's HLS is helpful in that it suggests that he may qualify for English-specific learning services. However, Heritage Language Surveys are only an indicative tool. While they can be extremely useful in highlighting *potential* ELLs, they cannot be used as an exclusive measure for language services enrollment.

If and when an HLS confirms that a student is new to English, he or she will be considered for language learning services. The enrollment specialist (in Newcomer settings, this is often the ELL department head, Student Assessment Liaison, or other trained personnel) carefully analyzes the data. Based on the parent's statement of Khaled's limited English proficiency, he will be referred for appropriate language testing.

Specific testing may vary from state to state or from district to district. Most schools employ WIDA ACCESS testing or a similar state/district approved measure. Regardless of testing instrument, timeliness is key. In fact, the U.S. Department of Education ensures that, "Local Education Agencies must identify in a timely manner ELL students in need of language assistance services."

It is critical to note that the Heritage Language Surveys (or any other form of registration questioning) is limited in its capacity. **That is, no information obtained through school enrollment can be used to evaluate, comment or report on legal immigration status.** Federal law strictly protects the rights of all children who are present in the U.S. to attend public school; and it conversely restricts school personnel from any inquiry or interference in legal immigration issues. There are many points to consider with regard to administering the Heritage Language Survey. Policies and procedures should be developed in advance of HLS administration. Let's walk through some of these essential questions together.

Heritage Language Survey Think Tank

Describe your schools' defined purpose for the Heritage Language Survey? In other words, how will you make this survey meaningful to students and parents?

_____
_____
_____
_____

Where on campus will the survey be completed?

_____

Who at your school will administer the Heritage Language Survey?

NAME	ROLE
_____	_____
_____	_____
_____	_____
_____	_____

Describe the training criteria for these individuals:

_____
_____
_____

In what languages will print copies of the HLS be immediately available?

_____
_____
_____

Additionally, the HLS can be orally translated into the following languages:

_____
_____
_____

If a student is highlighted as potentially eligible for ELL services, what English Language testing and placement models will your school use?

_____
_____
_____
_____

How is EL testing and placement information recorded and stored?

_____
_____
_____

Describe the continuous review process for ELL students:

_____
_____
_____

THE NEWCOMER FIELDBOOK

HERITAGE LANGUAGE SURVEY TEMPLATE

On the following pages you will find a template that can be used as a ready-to-roll version, or as a base line for creating a site-specific version.

There are a few things to note.

The first page of the HLS template is exactly as we have described, with essential questions for determining potential language services eligibility.

That's it. That's all you need.

However, you may find it useful to collect additional data. In that case, the additional pages of the survey will provide ideas with regard to collecting additional data and insights about the student and his or her family.

Additional data collection is optional for the school, depending on your school's needs and program goals. It is ideal to have as much information about a student's specific background and needs at the time of enrollment. The HLS addendum serves this purpose.

In any case, consistency is key. Make it a goal to have 100% incoming family participation in completing the questionnaire.

If you choose to ask for additional data, parents are not obligated to provide it. If parents choose to exercise their right to withhold data, this decision cannot effect child enrollment in any way.

EL YAAFOURI

Heritage Language Survey

_____
SCHOOL/CAMPUS

Student_____ID_____

> DISCLAIMER: Any information gathered is used for the sole purpose of student placement and determination of eligibility for specialized language services.
> Responses **cannot** be used to:
>
> ✖ Determine or question immigration status
> ✖ Contest students and/or family members in legal matters

Language Data

What language is most often spoken in the home?

☐ English ☐ Spanish ☐ Other _____

What language does the child speak most at home?

☐ English ☐ Spanish ☐ Other _____

What language did the child learn first?

☐ English ☐ Spanish ☐ Other _____

In what language would you like to receive information from the school (when possible)?

☐ English ☐ Spanish ☐ Other _____

Guardian_____ Signature_____

Date_____ Translator_____

© The Newcomer Fieldbook, 2017

Heritage Data

> THIS SECTION IS OPTIONAL. You can choose to provide additional information that will help the school staff to better understand and meet the learning needs of your child.
>
> CHOOSING NOT TO ANSWER WILL NOT EFFECT YOUR CHILD'S SCHOOL ENROLLMENT.

Country of Origin:
Secondary Countries:
Major cultural/religious observed dates in our home include:
In our experience, parent involvement at the school is considered: ☐ Usual   ☐ Unusual

For cultural/religious reasons, our family adheres to clothing protocol that includes:
For cultural/religious reasons, our family does *not* consume: ☐ pork   ☐ beef   ☐ cheese/dairy ☐ non-halal   ☐ other_____
Someone in our home drives a car: ☐ YES   ☐ NO
I would like to learn more about: ☐ Immunizations   ☐ Health/Dental Care ☐ After School Programs   ☐ School Sports   ☐ School Transportation ☐ Volunteering at School   ☐ Adult ESL   ☐ Public Transportation   ☐ Child Care ☐ Obtaining a Driver's License   ☐ Job Opportunities   ☐ Food/Clothing Assistance

© The Newcomer Fieldbook, 2017

Transportation

What does transportation look like for students at your school? Each district addresses the transportation needs of Newcomers in a different capacity. It is important to be clear about how your students will be serviced in their travel to and from school.

- How many students walk?
- How are in-boundary Newcomers and ELs bussed to school, if needed?
- How are out-of-boundary Newcomers and ELs bussed to school, if needed?
- Will bus services for out-of-boundary Newcomers and ELs be available after the student transitions from language learning services?
- Are students eligible for after-school bus transportation?
- By what means will students arrive to school for special occasions (performances, back-to-school night, parent-teacher conferences)?
- What transportation means are available to parents and caretakers of students?

Sometimes, it becomes necessary to be creative with regard to student and parent transportation. Occasionally, short-term solutions are required. Such is the case in the following example. Intention, forethought and clarity go a long way in any regard. What is your plan?

ATTENTION:

By law, information obtained for the purpose of school enrollment

CANNOT

be used to evaluate, comment or report on legal immigration status.

Sample posted sign, refugee and immigrant Newcomer enrollment.

THE NEWCOMER FIELDBOOK

SAMPLE NEWCOMER FAMILY TRANSPORTATION PROCEDURE

In certain cases, parents and other family members may require assistance in reaching the _____ campus for key events, such as conferences, school-based meetings, concerts and community-building occasions.

Protocol for alternative family transportation is as follows:

1) Students and families may eligible for alternative transportation if:
    a. Such a need has already been indicated on the Heritage Preference Data form
    b. Parents/adult family have indicated by voice or writing, to the homeroom teacher or office staff, that such a need exists
    c. Parents/adult family have previously notified Family Resource Center staff or community liaison that such a need exists.
2) For the _____ school year, the primary transportation zone includes _____.

    a. If 20 or more parents/family members are confirmed to attend a singular scheduled event, a _____ district bus will be reserved.
        i. District Transportation # _____
        ii. Cost $_____

    b. If less than 20 parents/family members are confirmed to attend an event, or if the visit is not part of a school wide function, alternative transportation will be requested.
        i. Mode of transport_____
        ii. Contact _____
        iii. Cost Range $_____

3) For the _____ school year, named secondary transportation zones are those outside of _____.
    a. For all students and family members in these areas, alternative transportation will be requested. *(See 2,B)*

Student Home Visits

Student home visits are a topic previously explored in *The Newcomer Student*. So, we won't go into great detail here. However, it is worth our time and energy to reiterate the importance of home visits, which are often overlooked tools for accentuating our students' at-school performance. In our work with Newcomer populations, home visits have an even greater significance. They act as a critical bridge between the classroom and the family, while providing deeper glimpses into the personalities, lives, challenges and talents of our learners.

As educators, we share in our commitment to support all learners on a path toward academic proficiency. The home environment is an essential, if often overlooked, indicator of a student's social and scholastic success. Teacher home visits are an effective means for connecting the home and school landscapes.

With regard to our work around diverse student populations, teacher home visits are of exceptional significance. They provide an essential link to students' families, granting insight into learners' lives, language, culture and needs. They also create and foster essential bonds of trust between the school and the home. Moreover, Newcomer families are more likely to become invested in school activities after a level of trust in a child's educational practitioner(s) has already been established. Home visits achieve the aim of cultivating parent-school relationships in organic, non-threatening ways.

A collective body of research demonstrates the overwhelming positive impacts of teacher home visits on EL scholastic achievement and healthy social integration. In fact, purposeful teacher home visits are linked to improved student academic progress, attendance rates, parent-school collaboration and volunteer participation. Data also indicates a strong correlation between school-wide teacher home visit initiatives and decreased disciplinary actions in schools. (Epstein & Sheldon, 2002) For our Newcomer families, this means that more families are engaged within the school community school entity, and more students are receiving the appropriate developmental supports both at school and at home. (Delgado-Gaitan, 2001)

Parents and caregivers typically experience a greater sense of comfort and confidence when meeting in the home. In this modified "conference" setting, caretakers may be less hesitant to share information that would be helpful to a child's teacher or school. Information gleaned from site visits can be used to create and implement strategic interventions for an individual student based on his or her specific academic, socio-emotional or integration needs.

FUNDS OF KNOWLEDGE

Perhaps most importantly, teacher home visits are opportunities for parents and students to share valuable funds of knowledge. *Funds of knowledge* make up the collective database of an individual's skills and understandings, as gained through life experience, education and practical application. Our Newcomer parents possess wisdom and life experience in areas that may include: economics, mathematics, heritage language proficiency, content expertise, trade capabilities and cultural knowledge. (Moll, Amanti, Neff and Gonzalez, 1992).

When practitioners are invited to discover and acknowledge parents' funds of knowledge, they are better able to prescribe home-learning plans that include and empower student guardians. Our culturally and linguistically diverse parents have much to offer and are eager to be a part of their child's school endeavors. To this end, the National Association of Educators (NEA) writes,

> "Parents became more actively involved in their child's education once they understood *how* to get involved and *what* the teacher wanted them to do. All parents want to be a part of their child's education but many of them, especially those from low socio-economic backgrounds or who speak a language other than English may not necessarily know the school's expectations nor how they can meet those expectations at home."

Site visits are a chance to discover of existing funds of knowledge in the home; clarify expectations for student learning; present opportunities for parent engagement; and intentionally use these assets in support of student learning.

In any case, don't wait! Get out there into your students' homes. Still need convincing? Project Appleseed shares,

> "Researchers…found evidence that home visits could increase student performance, jumpstart parent involvement, reduce discipline problems and increase overall positive attitudes toward school. If done correctly, a home visit program can give teachers, parents and students a better opportunity for connection, communication and collaboration."

A home visit checklist and template for recording home visits are located on the following pages. As for the home visit template, not all areas will need to be assessed. For example, sanitation factors may not be relevant, unless there are existing concerns related to a student's health, hygiene or well-being. You are encouraged to modify this template or create your own as you and your team discover action items that are of high importance or value to you.

Student Home Visits

- ☐ Plan to complete home visits with one or more adult peer practitioners. It is also a good idea to alert the school if you are planning to make a home visit.
- ☐ Ideally, the student will also be home. Do your best to ensure that this is the case.
- ☐ Try to visit as many students as possible, for as many reasons as possible. Home visits can address negative school behaviors, but they can (and should) occur for so many other positive reasons, including relationship building.
- ☐ Aim to schedule visits a week or two in advance.
- ☐ If the parents speak a language other than English, it may be helpful (and a great sign of respect) to learn a few key words or phrases, such as "hello" or "thank you" in their native language.
- ☐ Be observant of traditions or routines in the home, such as removing shoes at the door.
- ☐ Make a point to learn and use the names of family members.
- ☐ It may be helpful to bring a translator. If one isn't available, don't let that be a deal breaker! (In fact, I very rarely visit student homes with a translator.) Simple communication is almost always possible.
- ☐ Have a plan: decide what your objective, topic or aim of the visit will be.
- ☐ Brainstorm conversation starters before you go.
- ☐ Take mental notes, but hold off on recording information until after you leave.
- ☐ Relax! Home visits are meant to be enjoyable periods of time. In the vast majority of cases, families will be thrilled to have you as a guest- and you are likely to be the recipient of their sincere hospitality and generosity.

THE NEWCOMER FIELDBOOK

Student Home Visit Record

Student/Family Name: _____ Date: _____

School: _____ Guest/Visitor: _____

Reason for Visit: ☐ Family Outreach ☐ Orientation ☐ Translation ☐ Attendance ☐ Student Academics ☐ Student Behavior ☐ Celebration ☐ Health/Immunizations ☐ Homework Help ☐ Hygiene ☐ Parent Permissions ☐ Explain School Activities ☐ Attaining Resources ☐ Other

---

Home Environment Observations

☐ Apartment   ☐ Home   ☐ Other_____   ☐ Furnished   ☐ Unfurnished
Number of people living in home: Number of children living in home:
Other Information: ☐ Student sleeping area (shared/not shared) ☐ Functional bathroom(s) ☐ Kitchen Area ☐ Student work area ☐ Student reading materials ☐ Not Applicable/Observed
Notes:

Purpose of Visit

Participants:
Discussion:
Evidence:
Conclusion:

ACTION ITEMS	RESPONSIBLE PARTY	DEADLINE

© The Newcomer Fieldbook, 2017

4 THE ORIENTATION PROCESS

> Guiding Questions for Chapter 4:
> -- How do we go about the process of orientating new students and their families?
> -- How do we ensure that new families feel safe and welcomed in the initial moments?
> -- Have we brainstormed additional concerns or orientation steps that might influence the specific community that we serve?
> -- What steps can we take immediately that will create space for all members of our school or organization to become involved in orientating new students?
> -- What long term, positive implications can we expect that these moves will have for our school culture?
> -- Who are our available in-building and community liaisons that will assume responsibility for the development and implementation of these aims?
> -- How do we define and describe our student body and educational services to new families and community stakeholders?

Induction Programming

Induction programming is a best practices approach to Newcomer-ESL education, as it acts as an essential framework for positive, integrated socio-academic participation. These processes are a means of orientating the student to his or her new school surroundings. As an added component, Newcomer learners are introduced to essential concepts and understandings that are critical to success in a school-specific environment. Focus questions:

- *Who welcomes students and parents as they enter the school?*
- *Who is the first school contact for Newcomer families? The second?*
- *How are new students and parents introduced to the school and its staff? Are these processes amended when working with Newcomer families?*
- *How are all students, including Newcomers, made to feel welcomed and safe at school?*
- *What type of record-keeping systems ensures that no students are overlooked in the orientation process?*

Orientation systems can be complex or straightforward. They can stem from the office staff; may include teachers, parents, and other students; or may originate at a Welcome Center site. We'll focus our energies for this chapter on a few simple strategies that have a demonstrated effectiveness and are easy to implement. Then, if you're interested in going further in developing your own orientation plan, I encourage you to visit the additional resources at the end of this chapter.

PERSPECTIVE IS EVERYTHING

Did you ever have to move schools when you were younger? Or, what about that (huge) jump from the elementary grounds to the middle/high school campus? Overwhelming, right? I remember the first time I visited my high school. I was so convinced that I would never be able to find my classes. Or my locker. Or my friends. I actually had nightmares about it.

I spoke English. I had been in American schools my entire life. I had a network of peers that endured the transition with me. And, I was still shaking in my boots.

For a moment, consider the experience of school transition from a Newcomer perspective. We're not talking about moving across town, or even from another state. Imagine that *nothing is the same*. Nothing is predictable. Everything is lost in a cloud of newness: language, mannerisms, climate, clothing, school. *How would you react in this situation? What would you most wish for? What actions could a school take to help to ease your anxiety?*

Let's first examine the most critical aspects of school orientation. As you read through the following checklist, some of items might seem erroneous. *That's common sense*. Right- it's common sense from our perspective, based on our own previous exposure to localized normative values. But "normal" isn't normal everywhere.

Normal is a completely subjective concept.

And so, it is important to practice viewing our school and classrooms with raw eyes. We must remind ourselves that cultural misunderstandings are not a reflection of intelligence. They are a reflection of world experience- and that's a really cool thing! When I find myself in a cultural cross-tangle with one of my students, I like to ask my class: "Can you imagine if I visited your country? Would I know how to do everything right away? Could I speak your language with your grandmother or cook sambusa as well as your father?"

This usually garners some laughter and a hearty conversation about how I wouldn't even know that I was supposed to bow or kiss three times instead of shaking hands. "Nooooo waayyy!" But, when I ask if they would help me to feel safe by teaching me the things I would need to know, my students all eagerly agree! Just taking a moment to recognize our students' perspectives exposes our willingness to understand and relate to our students. This kind of effort can really break ground and lead to trust building.

Where can we anticipate questions, concerns or confusion? Here are some starters!

Newcomer Family Orientation Checklist

Logistics:
- ☐ Layout and map of the school
- ☐ School hours
- ☐ Student course schedule
- ☐ Meals at school (cafeteria options, subsidized meal applications)
- ☐ School transportation

Contact Information:
- ☐ Location and phone number of the main office
- ☐ Attendance line contact, if different
- ☐ Names and locations of key administrative personnel
- ☐ Name, location and contact information of teacher(s)
- ☐ Name and location of key resource personnel: nurse, ELD teacher, counselor, etc.

Policies:
- ☐ Immunizations
- ☐ Attendance
- ☐ Dress code (including winter and gym attire)
- ☐ Homework
- ☐ Supplies
- ☐ Behavior & Discipline
- ☐ Health and Wellness
- ☐ Cell Phones
- ☐ Safety (Weapons, Smoking, Alcohol, Drugs)
- ☐ Field Trips

© The Newcomer Fieldbook, 2017

Participation:
- ☐ Sitting for long periods
- ☐ Carpet meetings/sitting on the floor (where applicable)
- ☐ Lining up as a class
- ☐ Raising hand to speak
- ☐ Lockers (where applicable)
- ☐ Bell policy and tardiness
- ☐ Bathroom and hand washing routines
- ☐ Independent and group work routines

Events:
- ☐ Back-to-School Night
- ☐ Report Cards
- ☐ Parent Conferencing
- ☐ Concerts
- ☐ School dances
- ☐ International Night, if applicable

Participation:
Students:
- ☐ Sports and Recreation
- ☐ After School Tutoring
- ☐ Summer School

Parents:
- ☐ Classroom volunteer opportunities
- ☐ Field trip volunteer opportunities
- ☐ Adult ESL
- ☐ Translation services

© The Newcomer Fieldbook, 2017

THE NEWCOMER FIELDBOOK

ATTENDENCE POLICY

It is very important that your child attend school. It is the law. Sometimes, your child is unable to come to school. If your student cannot attend school, you must visit the school office or contact the school to provide a reason for the absence. The following school absences are usually "excused".

School Name	
Attendance Line	
Translator Line	
Website	

My child _____ cannot come to school today. He or she:

Is sick.

Has an appointment.

Has a problem at home.

Has a family holiday.

Is traveling.

Is moving.

© The Newcomer Fieldbook, 2017

VISUAL ORIENTATION HANDBOOK

I absolutely love this idea of a visual orientation handbook, shared with me by Silvia Tamminen, coordinator at the Aurora Public Schools (APS) Welcome Center in the Denver suburb of Aurora, Colorado.

The Aurora Public Schools (APS) Welcome Center supports one of the most diverse student populations in the state. In this capacity, families with school-aged children who are new to Aurora Public Schools and are also new to the English language are directly referred to the APS Welcome Center. Silvia and other staff members guide Newcomer families through the processes of student registration and school orientation.

Silvia, who is from Finland and speaks four languages herself, is a human rights professional with a concentration on refugee and migration issues. She came on board with the APS Welcome Center program in its inaugural season. She and her team built the organization from the bones up. The visual orientation handbook is among her creative, solution-seeking efforts.

The handbook is a non-consumable resource with a permanent home in Silvia's office. It is comprised of photos and illustrations and captioned with simple sentence explanations that lay out the expectations for a typical school day. For example, one picture shows a group of students sitting on the ground listening to a read-aloud. The caption reads, "Sometimes, students sit on the carpet during the school day."

This was an important inclusion, Silvia assured me. "Many times our parents cannot believe that their child would sit on the floor to learn. In some of their own countries, that would be very strange and maybe make a parent very angry." The purpose of this passage and photo was to ensure that all parents are informed that while learning does occur in traditional desk seating, it can also take other forms, such as group seating, learning outside of the classroom, and "crisscross" carpet engagement. This awareness can ease anxiety and foster transitional ease.

Other seemingly innocuous situations include: lunch, lockers, prompt arrival, and co-ed teaching staff, to name a few. Here- take a look for yourself. It's a comprehensive list!

Could you duplicate this resource at your site? As long as you have a camera and a few hours to spare, of course! (Just be sure to send out a thank you to the APS Welcome Center for the idea. Find them here: http://welcomecenter.aurorak12.org)

Quick List: What You Need to Know About School
Aurora Welcome Center: Refugee, Immigrant and Community Integration

Attendance

- According to the law in Colorado, all kids from age 6 to 17 have to go to school. In Aurora Public Schools, students can stay in school until they are 21. You do not have to pay for public education.
- Students need to attend classes every day. Parents are responsible for calling the school if their student is going to be absent. If the student is sick or has a doctor's appointment, the absence is excused. Parents are held accountable for their student's attendance. Remember that the student will not learn if they are not in class.
- Be on time. School start time is when the student needs to be in class.
- Follow the *school calendar* to know when there is no class for students.
- In case school is canceled because of snow, parents will be informed via phone call, TV, radio, and online. Most of the time students will still have school, even when it snows.
- K-8, middle schools and high schools have 'late start' on Wednesdays. During 'late start' school starts later than it normally does.

School Day

- Elementary school, middle school and high school have different start and end times. Each student has his or her own schedule.
- Girls and boys learn in the same classroom.
- Some elementary and middle schools require students to wear a uniform.
- Students have different teachers for different subjects. Students change classrooms during the day.
- Students have female (woman) and male (man) teachers. Call your teacher by his or her last name (example, Mr. or Mrs. Smith). Teachers want to help their students, and they want students to ask questions. Don't hesitate to reach out to your school staff if you have any question or concern.
- Parents are welcome to visit schools, meet with teachers, and spend a day at their child's school. Parents should stay involved with their student's education and attend parent-teacher conferences.
- Breakfast and lunch are served at school. There is always a non-pork meal option and a vegetarian meal option available. Students can also bring their own snack/meal to school.

Important Rules

- Update your child's immunization records with his or her school each time your child gets a new immunization.
- Always update your address and contact information on school records.
- Be respectful to *all* students and *all* school staff.
- There is no physical punishment at school, but there are other consequences for negative student behavior. Each school has a discipline policy.
- Students are responsible for doing their homework.
- Middle school and high school students have to carry their student I.D.s.
- Bullying is not allowed. If you experience bullying, tell an adult in your school right away!

Academic Success

- All English Language Learners (ELLs) will be placed in English Language Development (ELD) class to improve their English reading, writing, speaking and listening skills and to develop academic English.
- Students will receive a report card each quarter. Students are graded per grade level standard. Keep in mind that the grades will improve when the English language level increases!
- Every student will have to take standardized tests every year. The language barrier may affect newcomers' test scores, but each year you will see improvement. Always try your best at each test and assessment!
- It is important to graduate high school. Many jobs and colleges require a high school diploma.

Always do your best and ask if you don't know!

Co-ed Learning

Girls and boys are in the same classroom.

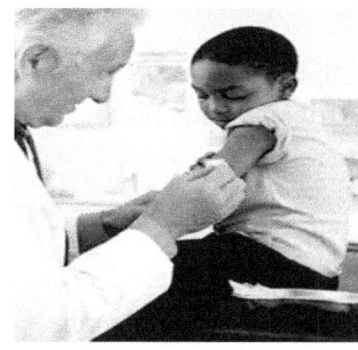

Update your student's immunization records with your child's school every time your student gets a new immunization.

Immunizations

  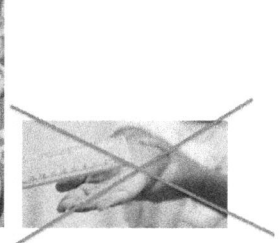

Physical Discipline

NO physical punishment allowed in school, but there are other consequences for student's behavior. Each school has a discipline policy.

Inclement Weather

In case school is cancelled because of snow, parents will be informed via phone call, TV, radio and online. Most of the time students still have school, even though it snows.

Aurora Public Schools Welcome Center
Silvia Tamminen, Aicha Nfaoui, Ana Pivaral, Ryan Lee, Nasibu Nizigiyimana, Mya Win, Khagendra Mishra, and Menghisteab Berhane

BUDDY PARTNERSHIPS

Buddy programs have a demonstrated effectiveness when it comes to: a) creating an environment of safety for new students; b) encouraging healthy relationships between students; and c) creating opportunities for guided support through peer mentorship and example.

These types of school-based efforts can be especially impactful in the context of orientating refugee and immigrant newcomer students. What I especially love about buddying is that the effects are almost always doubled, to the extent that both the mentor and the mentee receive direct socio-emotional benefits (as well as practical understanding) from these interactions.

Buddy partnerships take a different aesthetic from campus to campus. Some outside organizations provide very extensive, prescribed consulting services around buddy program implementation. If your organization happens to have access to these assets, great news! If not, don't worry. The Do-It-Yourself approach can produce similarly beneficial results.

Here are a few basic templates, just to get the wheels turning. If you choose to use any of these templates, they could certainly stand to be spruced up with some child-friendly graphics, colorful fonts or school logos, depending on the target age and interest group.

The templates include:

- BUDDY APPLICATION/SIGN UP FORM
- EMAIL/LETTER TO THE PARENTS and FAMILY
- INITIAL BUDDY MEETING SUGGESTED TALK POINTS

DO YOU WANT TO BE A "BUDDY"?

A buddy is a special friend who helps someone get used to a new place.

Have you ever been to a new place or a new school? Do you remember how you felt? Isn't it nice to have a friend to make you feel safe, show you important things and introduce you to new people? Buddies are an important part of our school community!

YOU could be that buddy! ☺

To be a buddy, you must first apply for the job. Then, you will be interviewed, so that we can find a "great-fit" buddy for you. Next, you will be trained for your special job, so that you can be the best buddy you can be. When new students arrive to our school, YOU could be asked to take action!

Would you make a great buddy? Fantastic!

Please fill out this form and return it to the main office by _____.

Student Name: _____Grade:_____

Parent Name: _____

Parent Phone/Email: _____

Parent Signature: _____

© The Newcomer Teacher, 2017

Hello, _____ and the _____ family!

You have a buddy! _____ has just moved to our area and is brand new to _____. He / She is very excited to have you as a friend!

Your buddy is from _____ and will be starting _____ grade this year.

Your buddy speaks a little bit / some / fluent English, as well as _____.

You will meet your new buddy on _____.

Here are some things you might want to talk to your buddy about:

- How to find important places in the school. Maybe you could draw a map or create one together!
- Tell about your favorite activities in school.
- Ask if they ride the bus, come in a car or walk to school
- Tell them how lunchtime works and that if you have the same lunchtime, you can sit together!
- Tell them about your "specials" times and what you do in those classes.
- Tell them about after school activities they might enjoy.
- Ask about their last school or the country they are from.
- Ask if they have any questions.

If your buddy is learning English, you can help by speaking clearly (not loudly). You might also use your hands when you speak, draw a picture, or show your buddy in person what you are describing.

We're so glad you signed up to be a buddy. We know that you will make our new student feel very welcome at our school. If you have any questions, please contact the main office directly.

Thank you,

_____

© The Newcomer Fieldbook, 2017

THE NEWCOMER FIELDBOOK

Getting to Know My Buddy

Who is my buddy?	My buddy's name is _____.
What is a buddy?	A buddy is a friend for someone who is new.
What does a buddy do?	1. Buddies show someone around a new school. 2. Buddies answer questions and help someone learn about a new place. 3. Buddies stay together with their new friend and help them to meet other students and teachers in the school.

Learn about my buddy!

My buddy is from _____.
My buddy's language is _____.
My buddy's favorite color is _____.
My buddy's favorite animal is _____.

© The Newcomer Fieldbook, 2017

NEWCOMER PROGRAM FLIERS

Program fliers announce the services provided by a Newcomer-inclusive school and clarify aims and statistics for community stakeholders. It is suggested that fliers include critical information about the school and its student population, including school mission and vision statements; culture or language demographics; key curriculum or strategy pieces; and relevant growth measures. What do you want new families and community members to know about your school, staff and students?

My first exposure to this idea came from the International Newcomer Academy (INA) in Fort Worth, Texas. This high school exclusively services Newcomers, as part of the Fort Worth Independent School District's on-ramp to mainstream transition for ELLs. INA has been providing language and acculturation services to students in the Fort Worth more than twenty-five years. They've devised some incredible systems, practices and resources along the way- among them, a comprehensive but concise International Newcomer Academy flier. That example is shared on the following page.

In working with Isabella Bird, the idea of a visual flier was adapted to reflect the culture and statistics specific to that site location. ELD Director Kim Hundley took the project on. Despite a packed school schedule, she managed to create the document over the course of a week using a simple Word flyer template. The result: an easy to read calling card for the school. Kim's example is also included on the following page.

These separate versions highlight different needs and vary in terms of format. However, they both achieve the same end goal of informing potential families and interested community members of a school's unique diversity and range of programming. What might this look like at your location? Already have one to share? Pass it on @RefugeeClassroom!

International Newcomer Academy is a one year Middle/High School educating newcomer students with little or no English language so that they will be successful in the Fort Worth Independent School District.

Mission Statement:
To engage English Language Learners in rigorous learning experiences that develop responsible, productive, and contributing citizens in a diverse society.

Placement at INA versus Language Centers
New arrivals to the U.S. go to the FWISD Student Placement Center (SPC) and are given a language fluency test (IPT) to determine their level of English Language Skills. Students needing intensive language support (level A and B) are sent to INA for their first year in FWISD. Afterwards, they go to their home school's Language Center. Students with higher levels (C and above) of English go directly into the Language Centers.

December Exit
Students enroll at INA throughout the school year. If a student arrives in the second half of a semester, they stay two more full semesters at INA. Due to this occurring in the fall semester and for those students arriving early in the spring semester, they will exit INA mid school year. These students are our December Exit group.

QTEL
Quality Teaching for English Learners Principles

Sustain Academic Rigor
- Promote deep disciplinary knowledge
- Engage students in generative disciplinary concepts and skills
- Engage students in generative cognitive skills (higher-order thinking)

Hold High Expectations
- Engage students in tasks that are high challenge and high support
- Engage students (and teachers) in the development of their own expertise
- Have clear criteria for high expectations
- Make criteria for quality work clear to all

Engage in Quality Interactions
- Engage students in sustained interactions with teacher and peers
- Focus interactions on the construction of knowledge

Sustain a Language Focus
- Promote language learning in meaningful contexts
- Promote disciplinary language use
- Amplify rather than simplify communications
- Address specific language issues judiciously

Develop Quality Curriculum
- Set long-term goals and benchmarks
- Use a problem-based approach with increasingly interrelated lessons
- Use a spiraling progression
- Make connections between subject matter and students' reality
- Build on students' lives and experiences

©2010 WestEd

International Newcomer Academy, 062
Fort Worth Independent School District
7060 Camp Bowie Boulevard
Fort Worth, Texas 76116
T: 817.815.5600

International Newcomer Academy
Fort Worth Independent School District

38 Different Countries
29 Different Languages

Rodrigo Durbin, Principal
rodrigo.durbin@fwisd.org

Kerwin Cormier, Assistant Principal
kerwin.cormier@fwisd.org

Amanda Bradley, Dean of Instruction
amanda.bradley@fwisd.org

Campus Challenges
As of November 15, 2016, student enrollment is 611. (Percentages listed below will fluctuate throughout the school year).
- **100%** of students are **ELLs** and non-English speaking at the time of enrollment.
- **100%** of students are **High At-Risk**.
- **43%** of students are either **Refugee, Unschooled, or Unschooled Refugee**.
- **38%** of students are **over-age & under-credited**.
- **13%** of students will stay for **2 years**. 87% will only stay for **one year**.
- **4%** of students will fall under INA's state **accountability**.

Overage Students
All high school students who enroll at INA start in the 9th Grade due to lack of credits awarded. Students who are older will attend Success High School after leaving INA to received accelerated instruction to graduate in less than the traditional time. These students are at a high risk of dropping out and need additional support and mentoring.

Language Education & Academic Preparation

A Specialized 2-year program, within INA, to prepare students with major gaps in education and pre-literate students for future career and academic success by providing an individually focused program for literacy and math that closes the gap in their educational background in a safe, nurturing environment.

The first year at INA, LEAP students receive intensive instruction in English, Reading, and Math. Their second year, they attend the regular grade level courses.

Current Enrollment (Nov 2016):
Total	611 students
Middle School	228 students
High School	383 students
Unschooled (SIFE)	15 students (3%)
Refugee	112 students (16%)
Unschooled Refugee	153 students (24%)
Ages 17-20	114 students (22%)
Age 16	98 students (16%)

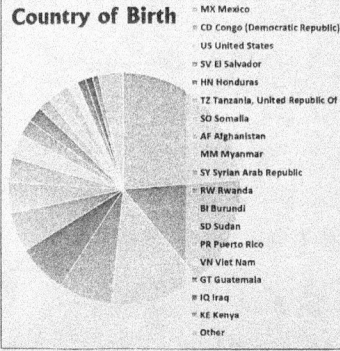

Country of Birth: MX Mexico, CD Congo (Democratic Republic), US United States, SV El Salvador, HN Honduras, TZ Tanzania, United Republic Of, SO Somalia, AF Afghanistan, MM Myanmar, SY Syrian Arab Republic, RW Rwanda, BI Burundi, SD Sudan, PR Puerto Rico, VN Viet Nam, GT Guatemala, IQ Iraq, KE Kenya, Other

Languages:
Arabic	French	Krio	Shan
Burmese	Haitian-Creole	Kunam	Somali
Chin	Ibembe	Malay	Spanish
Chintedim	Karen	Mandarin	(Ki)Swahili
Dari	Karenni	Moro	Tigrinya
Dinka	Kinyarwanda	Nepali	Vietnamese
Farsi	Kirundi	Pashto	Zomi

QTEL Coaches & PDers
Quality Teaching for English Learners

After receiving 3 years of intensive Professional Development from WestEd's QTEL, INA continues to support the professional development of our teachers through QTEL coaching and continued PD provided by 3 teachers who are QTEL certified Professional Developers. INA currently has 8 QTEL Coaches with 2 being QTEL PDer certified.

Staff: 42 Teachers
- ESL/English I 8
- Reading 8
- Math/Algebra I 8
- Social Studies/World Geography. 6
- Science/Integrated Physics & Chemistry. 6
- Reading Specialist 1
- I-Ready Lab 1
- Art 1
- Touch Systems Data Entry 1
- Physical Education 1
- Health 1
- Teaching Assistants 5

Counseling
High School   Ms. Shuler   817.815.5615
Middle School   Ms. Dibi   817.815.5616
Interventionist   Ms. Stone   817.815.5534

Parent Resources
Parent Coordinator   817.815.5693
Social Worker   Mrs. Al-Atrash
    Mrs. Rosas

Credit: International Newcomer Academy, Texas

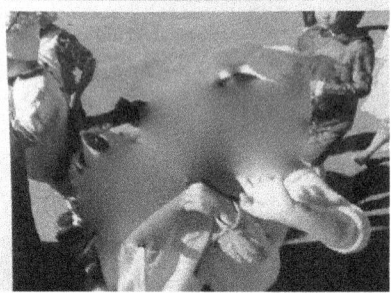
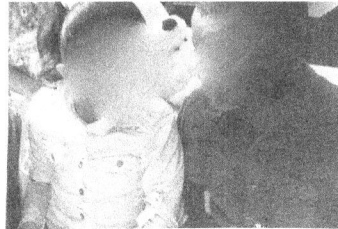

Credit: Isabella Bird Community School, Colorado

5 DIAGNOSTIC & PLACEMENT TESTING

> **Guiding Questions for Chapter 5:**
> -- What state/district protocol for diagnostic assessment is already in effect?
> -- What additional assessments would make sense at our location?
> -- What additional diagnostic or placement tools would make sense for our students at our location?
> -- What is the process for ensuring that such measures are district/state approved?
> -- How are school SALs (Site Assessment Liaisons) and teachers trained to conduct such assessments?
> -- What steps can we take immediately that will ensure that proper diagnostic protocol is being followed and documented correctly every time?
> -- What will be our course of action if and when a student's diagnostic placement does not align with demonstrated classroom capabilities?

An Author Note on Assessment

Assessment of ELLs, including Newcomer ELLs, is a complicated ball of wax. While a multitude of texts exist on the subject of formal testing, research on the subject of language-based assessment remains limited. We are writing this new world as we go.

We will do our best to explore the world of modern ELL evaluative instruments. It is important that we develop as clear an understanding of these mechanisms as possible. Still, there is something more important than any test feature we can learn about.

The child.

No measure of assessment can accurately capture the abilities and characteristics of an individual student. No instrument can offer a composite picture of a child, with all of his or her unique qualities, skills or potential. A test cannot reveal a child's curiosity, or his or her determination or drive to learn.

A test is a tool with limited and often flawed capabilities that, in the best-case scenarios, allows us some insight into a learner's thinking. That's it.

So, while we will spend the next chapters diving into the labels that we create for our students, I ask that you pause throughout to remind yourself that labels allow us to communicate with each other as educators. They do not define a child.

In fact, data reveals that a significant number of ELLs are misclassified via traditional assessments. As a result, many learners are not receiving appropriate language services. They may be denied access to essential programming, or they may be receiving too much of a good thing. Take the labels lightly.

A whole child approach to assessment requires that we collect and review outcomes from a variety of performance measures. One data point is not enough. This body of evidence should include both formative and summative evaluation points, and should make room for teacher, parent and social worker/counselor input. It should also include student work samples from district-selected, school-selected, teacher-selected and student-selected tasks.

Take these assessments as a launch point, as a probable indication of where our students fall on the language-learning spectrum. Employ test results as a means of informing instruction. But remember that the best course in learning about a child is also the most trusted and time-tested: spend quality learning time with him or her.

Diagnostic & Placement Assessment for ELLs

Of all the components of refugee Newcomer education, assessment for ELLs has always been the most daunting for me, personally. Perhaps this is because the testing spectrum is so vast. Or, because I know that assessing English proficiency for non-native speakers is a slippery slope at best. Perhaps, it is because I don't view student testing as fun or engaging (albeit necessary, I admit).

Here's what I really think. I think that I avoid the subject of assessment because it's a world of five thousand acronyms, and my brain can handle a grand total of three per sentence (we'll top that a few times in this section).

The goal here is to create a little bit of clarity around assessment instruments for ELLs. You'll likely feel overwhelmed in piecing through this section. Though condensed and simplified, the labyrinth still exists. Take a few breaths, set it down, and please, don't take it out on the messenger!

Here's a scenario: during the registration process, a student has been recommended for further consideration of ELL services eligibility. So, now what?

This is a broad question, so here's the broad answer: he or she will be assessed to determine the level of English language proficiency and, subsequently, eligibility for ELL services. Of course, as we dig into language testing and student placement, we find a web of assessment possibilities. The tools that a school employs for language testing ELLs are the result of national, state, district and site-based preference or mandate.

At the national level, the NCLB Act mandates annual language proficiency testing for ELLs. It also requires that, "English Language Proficiency (ELP) assessments include four modalities (reading, writing, speaking, and listening), incorporate the concept of academic language, and align the content of ELP assessments with the states' ELP standards."

At the statewide level, the Elementary and Secondary Education Act (ESEA), serves to officially define ELL and LEP (Limited English Proficiency) students. Decisions about how those definitions are interpreted and acted upon vary from state to state. As the National Research Council (NRC) clarifies, "the act leaves it to states to operationalize the definition and to determine procedures for identifying students in need of Title III services."

Entry and exit criteria also vary significantly from state to state. The range of these decisions has implications for students and teachers. Criteria and placement measures affect the total number of students receiving Title III language learning services. One NRC report states that,

> "Some states have relatively stringent entry criteria and relatively lenient exit criteria, which means they are providing Title III services only for students most in need. Other states have more lenient entry criteria and more stringent exit criteria, which means they are providing services to many students with English language difficulties and retaining them in the classification until they are ready to function without specialized language and instructional support services."

Ultimately, students who are ultimately designated as English Language Learners (ELLs) will fall into one of two categories:

- NEP: Non-English Proficient
- LEP Limited English Proficient

In the majority of U.S. schools, ELL designation requires a two-part protocol:

1. A heritage language survey (also called home language survey/home language questionnaire) is completed by the incoming family at the time of enrollment.
2. Students who are identified as probable ELLs based on the HLS data are to be tested to determine the existing level of English Language proficiency and to make recommendations for appropriate class placement.

CREATING CONTEXT

Diagnostic assessments for probable ELLs fall into overarching categories: those initiated pre-NCLB (No Child Left Behind) and those created post-NCLB/Title III. These two eras differ significantly in terms of theory, administration, and state-to-state consensus. It can be argued that overall reliability and validity of testing measures are more advanced in the second group, although the idea of validity in assessing language skills among English Language Learners is still a contested one.

We'll take a moment to become acquainted with the NCLB/Title III mandates. The

Educational Testing Service summarizes them nicely; we'll use that description to guide our work.

> *"Under NCLB, the academic progress of ELLs is assessed in two ways:*
>
> *(1) Under Title I, ELLs are one of the mandated subgroups whose test scores are used to determine whether schools and districts are meeting the goals for adequate yearly progress (AYP) based on state-level performance standards established for their students. ELLs are held to the same expectations as other subgroups regarding participation and attainment of proficiency on selected content area assessments (although ELL students are allowed a grace period during which the scores will not count).*
>
> *(2) Under Title III, ELLs must also demonstrate progress in attaining English language proficiency."*

LEADING UP TO "NO CHILD LEFT BEHIND"

Pre-NCBL (No Child Left Behind) testing measures include such assessments as the Idea Proficiency Test (IPT), Language Assessment Scales (LAS), Basic Inventory of Natural Language (BINL), the Woodcock-Muñoz Language Survey, and the Bilingual Syntax Measure (BSM). Dr. Jamal Abedi, who details the subject at length, informs that, " the pre-NCLB assessments were developed by different organizations at different times based on different needs and requirements."

Abedi later points to research that "found major differences between these tests with respect to their purpose, age and language group, administration, cost, items, scoring, test design, theoretical foundation, reliability, and validity of the tests." In short, inconsistency across a national spectrum is one hallmark of pre-NCLB diagnostic language assessment.

The two eras also diverge with respect to the weight of basic interpersonal communication skills (BICS) and cognitive academic language proficiency (CALP) on the ELL assessment process. Pre-NCLB measures are heavily based in common conversational ability, or the BICS portion of language production. Post-NCLB instruments are more likely to include and assess CALP with intentionality.

AFTER "NO CHILD LEFT BEHIND"

Post-NCLB/Title III initiatives seek to clarify the interpretation of "valid and reliable" language proficiency testing through the process of: a) aligning assessment to state ELP standards; and b) encouraging state-to-state collaboration and streamlining of assessment tools. Newly forged multi-state language consortiums drew focus to four distinct language learning capacities- listening, speaking, reading and writing- and sought to categorize proficiency according to specified rubrics within these modalities.

WIDA and similar frameworks are representative of the post-NCLB shift. In 2003, eight member states of the WIDA Consortium joined together to create the English Language Proficiency standards now associated with ACCESS. The National Research Council confirms that, "In developing the standards, the consortium wanted to ensure two essential elements:

(1) a strong representation of the language of state academic standards across the core content areas (language arts, math, science, social studies, and the classroom setting); and

(2) consensus by member states on the components of the ELP standards. As new states have joined the consortium, teams of researchers have continued the process by conducting alignment studies between the WIDA standards and a state's content standards."

Additionally, post-NCLB efforts draw focus to "academic English". Academic English may be defined as, "the oral, written, auditory, and visual language proficiency required to learn effectively in schools and academic programs," according to the Glossary of Education Reform. On post-NCLB instruments, Jamal Abedi notes that, "many of the newly developed measures of ELP are based on academic English to facilitate learning content knowledge."

Testing measures for ELLs have evolved significantly in recent years. Still, we must keep in mind that even the most progressive instruments of student evaluation are not absolute. Many questions remain: What is the appropriate balance between assessing academic language and testing content understanding? What factors determine validity and reliability? How is the correlation between language proficiency testing and state ELP standards defined?

Another point of concern has to do with the fact that many incoming students are impacted by personal factors that can have implications for assessment. Few, if any, of these considerations are represented in the context of traditional language proficiency testing. Nonetheless, these items do influence the validity of students' testing outcomes, especially as they relate to refugee Newcomers. Here's a short list:

- level of formal education;
- level of heritage language literacy;
- length of interrupted schooling;
- level of previous exposure to standardized testing;
- level of acculturation. (ETS, 2015)

LOOKING AHEAD: ESSA (Every Student Succeeds Act) & ELLs

What do new ESSA regulations mean for English Language Learners? U.S. News reported in 2016 that, "For the first time, minority students- Black, Hispanic, Asian-American and Native American students- now make up a *majority* of our public school students." Most U.S. schools now enroll at least one English Language Learner. ESSA addresses this. But, we'll need to reverse first.

In 1965, under the leadership of Lyndon B. Johnson, Congress passed the Elementary and Secondary Education Act (ESEA), the purpose of which ensures access to quality education for all children living in the U.S. This law was rooted in Johnson's firm belief that, "full educational opportunity [should be] our first national goal." No other piece of federal legislation has had such far-reaching or long-lasting impressions on education in the United States.

The No Child Left Behind Act (2002) falls under the umbrella of ESEA. Two separate provisions under ESEA/NCLB legislation have historical implications for English Language Learners. The first is "Title I", which aims to regulate allocations of funding and resources to the benefit of schools and school districts with high percentages of low-income populations. Title III is a separate ESEA provision that was reauthorized under NCLB that "aims to ensure that English Language Learners (ELLs) and immigrant students attain English proficiency and meet the state's challenging academic achievement standards." (Texas Education Agency, 2016)

Then, ESSA came along. President Barack Obama signed the Every Student Succeeds Act (ESSA) on December 15, 2015. ESSA is an extension of the visions outlined by ESEA and NCLB, but with a clearer intent to prepare students for post-high school success. The new act replaces and revises the NCLB reauthorization of ESEA. As explained by the U.S. Department of Education, "this bipartisan measure reauthorizes the 50-year-old Elementary and Secondary Education Act (ESEA), the nation's national education law and longstanding commitment to equal opportunity for all students."

Accountability is the calling card of the new Every Student Succeeds Act. ESSA is designed to increase and effectively measure school and district accountability in meeting the specific needs of all students, including English Language Learners. This is achieved through a process of requiring that all students in U.S. schools are taught to rigorous, identifiable standards and that all students are routinely assessed by measures that align to states' academic standards.

The act also puts the states in greater control of the schools and districts within their jurisdiction. Each state is expected to define high-level academic standards for all grades, across all content areas. States are also charged with managing student assessments and ensuring that standardized testing measures are aligned with state standards. Finally, each state is responsible for overseeing all measures of accountability with regard to the teachers, administrators, schools and school districts as they aim to increase opportunities for student success.

In defining accountability, ESSA inserts additional provisions not included in NCLB. For example, ESSA-defined school and district accountability measures make room for mandatory indicators that are specific to English language proficiency (ELP) growth and achievement across the four domains of listening, speaking, reading and writing. Schools and districts are also required to incorporate at least one school quality and/or student success indicator.

ESSA is designed in a way that places emphasis on integrated systems of learning. The previously mentioned ELP aims are restated in a way that embeds them in the overarching principals of Title I. Therefore, they have been moved from ELL-specific Title III and incorporated into Title I.

For clarification, they include:

- Identification and intervention of ELLs
- Alignment of ELP standards to state standards
- Alignment of ELP assessments to ELP standards
- Defined accountability indicators for ELP goals

Finally, ESSA elaborates on NCLB's vision for parent engagement. The updated act clarifies the expectations for Local Education Agencies (LEA) with regard to ELLs. They must:

- Provide for timely notification to parents related to ELL identification and school placement
- Actively advocate for and maintain records related to parent participation, including parent meetings and conferencing
- Report to the state yearly data around ELL academic and language proficiency growth

New revisions are expected in the years to come. For now, we cozy up to ESSA, which represents the most comprehensive federal governance over the quality of ELL education to date. Scott Sargrad of U.S. News reported that, "Now, under the Every Student Succeeds Act, all schools have to demonstrate that they are improving the English language proficiency of their English Language Learners. Importantly, these changes signal to states that helping English Language Learners gain the skills they need to be successful in academic classes must be a priority." Music to our ELL educators' ears.

GRADE LEVEL DETERMINATIONS

With regard to grade level placement, Newcomers are almost always placed according to the age as determined by the child's birth certificate, or other qualifying document. Very rarely, and based on a range of evidence that includes parent approval, a Newcomer child may be place at a grade level that is deemed more developmentally appropriate than the age-based assignment.

However, the National Clearinghouse for English Language Acquisition (NCELA) notes, "The [school] staff must take into consideration an unusual mix of factors which are often at odds with one another including age, language proficiency, literacy in native language, years of schooling, and familiarity with school and society."

Therefore, *placement* of Newcomers is a response to the following questions:
- In which class grade does the child belong based on his or her legal age?
- Will the child receive additional ELL services?
- Does the extent of language services eligibility qualify the student for Newcomer programming?
- What level within available Newcomer programming is most appropriate for the learner?

Enrollment Flow Chart, ELD Services

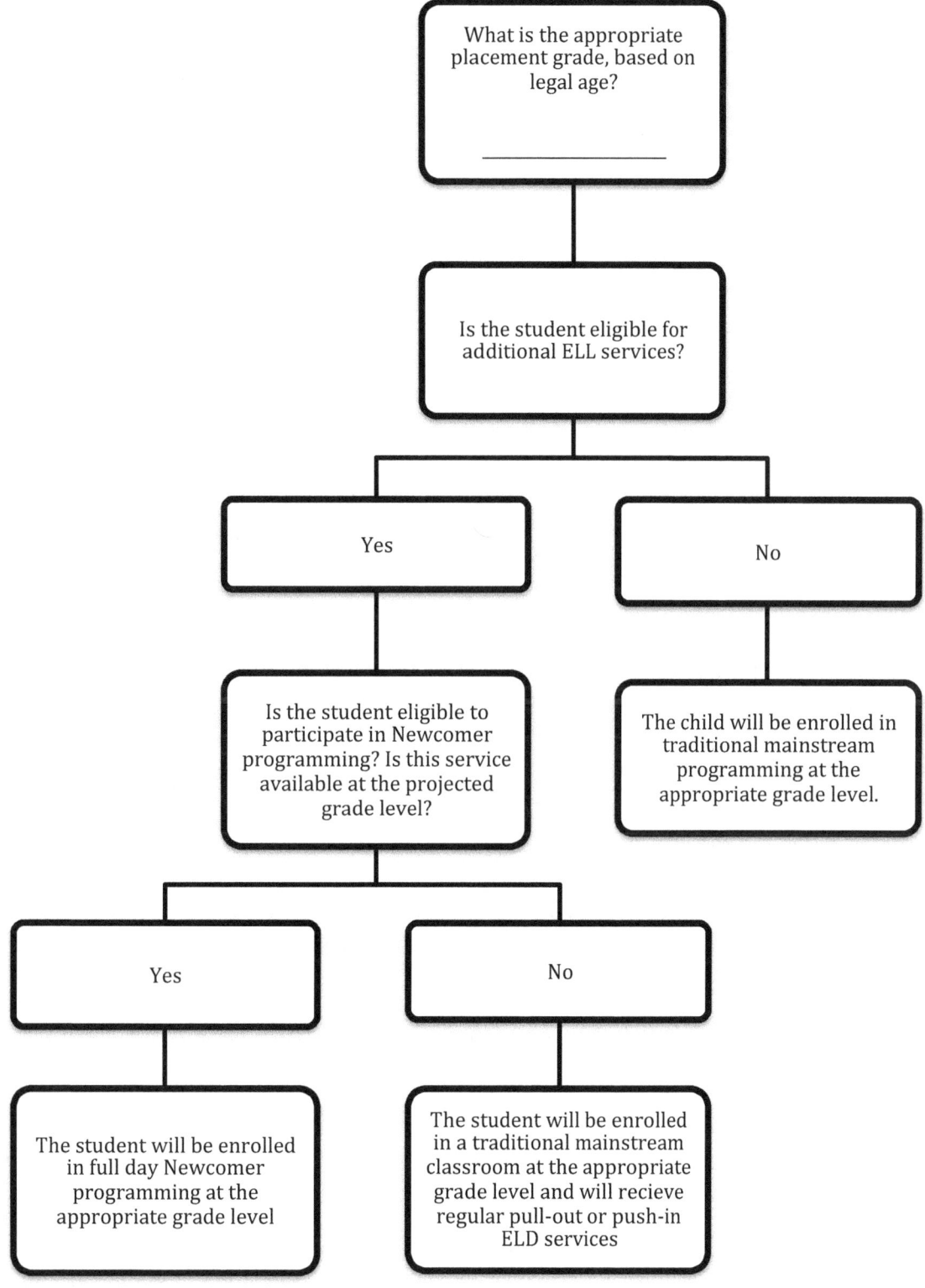

WHAT ABOUT MY SCHOOL'S ASSESSMENTS?

In the post-NCLB/Title III push, we are seeing a resolve toward creating assessments that are "valid, reliable, research-based instruments… based on TESOL standards, WIDA standards, and CCSS, and teacher friendly." (Stanford English Language Proficiency Test 2LPT, 2016). Pre-NCLB measures have been updated to comply with Title III requirements, incorporate CALP output and demonstrate compatibility with a comprehensive range of modern standards.

Most assessment outcomes are now banded by language proficiency level. The labels to these bands vary from one instrument to another. However, the general interpretation is the same; placements occur on a scale that includes pre-functional, beginning, intermediate and advanced language proficiency.

Following is a quick summary of the most widely accepted and district-approved tests for ELLs:

WIDA ACCESS for ELLs- Modalities: Listening, Speaking, Reading and Writing. Purpose: Annual assessment. Progress monitoring designated ELLs within WIDA Consortium states.
https://www.wida.us/assessment/ACCESS20.aspx

W-APT [WIDA]- Modalities: Listening, Speaking, Reading and Writing. Purpose: Designation, Placement. ELLs within WIDA Consortium states.
https://www.wida.us/assessment/ACCESS20.aspx

Alberta K-12 ESL Proficiency Benchmarks- Modalities: Listening, Speaking, Reading and Writing. Purpose: Diagnosis, Identification, Placement, Progress Monitoring, Exit.
http://www.learnalberta.ca/content/eslapb/search.html

Stanford English Language Proficiency Test 2 (SELP) [Pearson] - Modalities: Listening, Speaking. Purpose: Diagnosis, Identification, Placement, Progress Monitoring, Exit.
http://www.pearsonenglishlearningsystem.com/assessment

Language Assessment Systems Links (LAS Links) Areas [CTB/McGraw-Hill, updated LAS]: Modalities: Listening, Speaking, Reading, and Writing. Purpose: Diagnosis, Identification, Placement.
http://www.datarecognitioncorp.com/Pages/default.aspx?p=products&productFamilyId=454&productId=32348

Comprehensive English Language Learning Assessment (CELLA) [English Proficiency for All Students (EPAS) consortium]- Modalities: Listening, Speaking, Reading, and Writing. Purpose: Diagnosis, Identification, Placement, Progress Monitoring, Exit.
http://www.awschooltest.com/comprehensive-english-language-learning-assessment-cella-online-cms-84

English Language Development Assessment (ELDA) [Council of Chief State School Officers]- Modalities: Listening, Speaking, Reading, and Writing. Purpose: Diagnosis, Identification, Placement, Progress Monitoring, Exit. http://www.ccsso.org/Resources/Programs/English_Language_Development_Assessment_(ELDA).html

Woodcock-Muñoz Language Survey-Revised [Houghton Mifflin Harcourt]- Modalities: Listening, Speaking, Reading, and Writing. Purpose: Diagnosis, Identification, Placement, Progress Monitoring, Exit. http://www.hmhco.com/hmh-assessments/bilingual/woodcock-munoze

Common State Assessments:

Arizona English Language Learner Assessment (AZELLA) [version of SELP]

California English Language Development Test (CELDT)

Colorado English Language Assessment (CELA) [version of LAS LINKS]

New York State English as a Second Language Test (NY-SESLAT) [Pearson]

Texas English Language Proficiency Assessment System (TELPAS) [Texas Education Agency]

Additional Resources:

http://ecs.force.com/mbdata/mbquestNB2?rep=ELL1403

https://www.ets.org/s/about/pdf/ell_guidelines.pdf

https://wida.us

6 PROGRESS MONITORING, ACCOMMODATIONS & PROGRAM EXIT

> ### Guiding Questions for Chapter 6:
> -- What strategies do we currently have in place to monitor our students' progress?
> -- What assessment resources are specifically dedicated for ELLs? How do we honestly rate the effectiveness of these instruments?
> -- What can we add, subtract or modify to increase validity and relevancy of data?
> -- In what ways will progress monitoring data on ELLs drive instruction in our building? Who is accountable for ensuring that this occurs?
> -- Can we identify specific state/district exit criteria for ELLs? Do we hold our students to additional measures of accountability and readiness in making decisions around re-designation?
> -- How do we define our student evaluation team? What roles and expectations do administrators/SALs/teachers have in these processes?
> -- Who are our available in-building and community resources that can contribute to the development and success of our program?

Section A: Progress Monitoring for ELLs

It is necessary to have a means of assessing ELL students as they move through the various stages of language development and academic participation. This is doubly important, as traditional markers for grade level growth are unlikely to service refugee Newcomer language learners. A variety of tools exist for the purpose of progress monitoring of ELLs.

WIDA-ACCESS is a prominent authority on this topic, and the WIDA-ACCESS tools are used by many as a resource for evaluating newcomer students' language acquisition. As part of the ACCESS framework, WIDA offers a clear rubric that teachers can use to evaluate student placement and progress in the classroom setting.

The indicators within each WIDA platform and across each of the language domains can be somewhat vague. Nonetheless, they do offer a guideline that promotes at least relative consistency. These tools can be found free of charge on the WIDA website.

Canada has also produced exemplary diagnostic and tracking tools for language learners. The Alberta K-12 Proficiency Standards are an especially comprehensive package. They provide practitioners with specific and detailed progress markers across all content areas, which are then further broken down into the domains of listening, speaking, reading and writing.

The Alberta ESL Benchmarks can be used as a stand-alone tool or as an effective crosscheck for both WIDA and WIDA-alternative assessment measures. The Alberta ESL Benchmarks are available at no cost and can be searched by grade level, domain and subject. This resource is located at http://www.learnalberta.ca/content/eslapb/index.html.

Technology-based tools can be employed to a similar end. EduSkills, for example, works directly with school districts to effectively input, monitor and safely store student data. It offers a specialized user interface that allows teachers to respond to questions about students' language capabilities in the classroom context. The EduSkills system incorporates this educator insight in establishing a probable English language level for a given student. Then, it offers aligned instructional tools to promote progression toward the next language level, with an end goal of proficiency.

Most of the placement assessments mentioned in the previous chapter also offer a means for monitoring student growth toward language proficiency. In these circumstances, it will be necessary to refer to product details, or to state or district websites for clarification of progress monitoring procedures for ELLs. In any case, yearly monitoring of designated ELLs is a school's legal responsibility.

NEWCOMER LEVELED FOCUS AREAS

Some programs level Newcomer students as a means of providing targeted instructional design and support. Newcomer leveling can take a variety of forms. It may also be structured differently from district to district and from one campus to another.

Leveling may occur on a scale that includes beginning, intermediate and advanced. Or, in the case of WIDA and the Alberta ESL Benchmarks, on a tiered scale of language proficiency across the four modalities of speaking, listening, reading and writing. For the purpose of clarity and simplicity, we will partition Newcomer ELs into three broad categories, or domains, of proficiency. In a school that provides leveled Newcomer coursework, these domains may translate into separate Newcomer classes across each grade level.

Indicators within a level are not always exclusive to one level domain. Similarly, students may demonstrate a range of skills that may overlap two or all three leveled domains. Generally, the domain in which a student achieves the greatest number of indicators is the dominant, or placement, level.

Some schools offer Level 1 and Level 2 Newcomer coursework. Thus, Level 1 students will achieve or work toward indicators in Domain 1, and may achieve some indicators in Domain 2. Level 2 learners would demonstrate capacities in Domains 2 and 3. Benchmark indicators can be integrated across leveled domains to confirm placement and track growth.

The following three-tiered version is a condensed system for approximating language ability level, tracking student progress and recommending students for transition or program exit. As students work across the domains, they develop the skills and resources necessary to fully participate in traditional mainstream classrooms. The Newcomer Leveled Focus charts act as at-a-glance checklists for essential instructional aims and key student understandings.

Domain 1 Focus Areas:

Beginning Participation Cues

1. Follow basic one and two step directions
2. Participate in group discussions and projects
3. Adhere to daily schedule and routine, including homework routines
4. Explore books for enjoyment
5. Learn and practice key host culture social norms
6. Introduce self
7. Express basic needs and wants

Beginning Literacy & Conventions Cues

8. Recognize letters and letter sounds
9. Demonstrate basic phonemic awareness/phonics skills, including blends
10. Invent spelling through phonemic reasoning
11. Spell basic consonant-vowel-consonant (CVC) words
12. Identify and produce short and long vowel sounds
13. Decode Tier 1 words
14. Recognize and utilize basic plural structures
15. Appropriately capitalize sentences and "I" pronouns
16. Appropriately utilize he/she and him/her gender pronouns
17. Appropriately use basic punctuation: periods, question marks, exclamation marks

Beginning Production Cues

18. Listen to and mimic stories and non-fiction literature
19. Mimic familiar adult and/or peer speech
20. Make basic predictions about plot outcomes
21. Identify main characters and setting
22. Communicate through simple noun-verb structures
23. Compare and contrast using Venn diagrams
24. Retell or draw stories with limited detail and beginning/ middle/ end
25. Construct simple sentences (with frames when needed)
26. Write, edit and publish single and multi-sentence writing compositions, with extensive supports

Domain 2 Focus Areas:

Intermediate Participation Cues

1. Follow directions, up to five steps
2. Participate in and lead group discussions and projects
3. Adhere to daily schedule and routine, including homework routines
4. Practice beginning time and resource management abilities
5. Practice problem solving capabilities, with supports
6. Develop and expand understanding of social norms, including body language and facial expressions

Intermediate Literacy & Conventions Cues

7. Demonstrate an understanding of phonics concepts
8. Recognize and utilize irregular plural structures
9. Identify root words and beginning prefix and suffix structures
10. Identify and correctly use digraphs and possessives
11. Identify and use entry-level academic vocabulary
12. Appropriately syllabicate words
13. Decode and spell Tier 2/3 words
14. Make predictions and inferences and identify sequence in a text
15. Appropriately capitalize proper nouns
16. Appropriately use punctuation, including: periods, question marks, exclamation marks, commas, and apostrophes
17. Develop a basic understanding of common contractions
18. Use dictionaries/picture dictionaries to decipher word meanings

Intermediate Production Cues

19. Communicate using noun-verb, adjective and adverb structures
20. Listen to and read along with stories and non-fiction literature
21. Read and report on leveled readers (approaching grade level)
22. Identify characters, setting, theme and motive
23. Retell stories with extensive detail and complete sentence responses
24. Oral storytelling with beginning, middle and end
25. Construct sentences with conjunctions, with minimal support
26. Construct single paragraph writing samples that include an introduction, details and conclusion
27. Write, edit and publish beginning writing compositions, with supports

Domain 3 Focus Areas:

Advanced Participation Cues

1. Follow multi-step directions
2. Participate in and lead group discussions and projects
3. Efficiently solve problems in independent and group capacities
4. Effectively manage time and resources
5. Reading grade level and above grade level texts

Advanced Literacy & Writing Cues

6. Understand spelling patterns and decode complex words
7. Appropriate capitalization of titles and first words inside quotation marks
8. Appropriate use of punctuation, including: periods, question marks, exclamation marks, commas, apostrophes, quotation marks, colons, semi-colons
9. Identify and correctly use general homonyms
10. Appropriately use contractions, possessives, and plural possessives
11. Explore sarcasm and humor in language
12. Identify and appropriately use metaphors, similes, and idioms
13. Understand and utilize grade-appropriate academic language

Advanced Production Cues

14. Communicate using advanced noun-verb, adjective and adverb structures and clear pronunciation
15. Read and report on leveled readers (high approaching or at grade level)
16. Paraphrase fiction and non-fiction text
17. Compare and contrast orally and in writing using examples and details from text
18. Compare and contrast different types of literature and/or different stories from the same author
19. Construct multi-paragraph writing samples that include an introduction, details and conclusion
20. Research and quote essential texts related to a topic of study
21. Develop arguments based on evidence and reasoning

Notes on Newcomer Leveling

At every level, basic principals of effective Newcomer instruction do apply.

AIM TO	AVOID

Set the bar high- students will reach where you place it.
 	
 Employ grade-level content texts and materials, encouraging students to:
 	
 • Make meaning from lesson objectives to drive learning
 • Follow along with oral reading
 • Demonstrate conceptual understanding through graphic organizers, maps, and labeled illustrations
 • Define key vocabulary and/or build personal glossaries for story or unit
 • Participate in content-specific cooperative talk structures with peers
 • Access grade level content learning through sheltered instruction techniques, to include the use of:
   o *Visual cues and realia*
   o *Physical manipulatives*
   o *Graphic organizers, timelines, charts, maps*
   o *Illustrations or collages with appropriate labels*
   o *Story sequence maps*
   o *Rubrics and student samples/model work*
   o *Non-verbal gestures, facial expressions/body language*
   o *Demonstrated understanding through art, drama, or song*
   o *Guided peer discussion*
   o *Activating background knowledge*
	Setting the bar too low- students will achieve it.
	
	 • Assuming that all international students require targeted English language instruction.
	 • Straying from grade level content
	 • Objectives that are not purposeful, unclear or inconsistent
	 • Worksheets
	 • Exclusively independent work, as these tasks have the capacity to isolate learners.
	 • Watering down texts and activities- language learners will begin to develop key concepts and ideas, even before fluency is established
	 • Unnecessary teacher talk. Strive to maintain a 1:2 or 1:3 ration of teacher-talk time (TTT) to student-talk time (STT) or better.
	 • Maintaining language supports after the point that they are no longer necessary.

NEWCOMER-SPECIFIC TRACKING RESOURCES

Sometimes, we just wish to be able to evaluate and monitor our Newcomers for our own classroom purposes. Certainly, we all hope to achieve an accurate snapshot of our students in a certain place and time in their cognitive development, so that we can effectively guide them toward the next mark of self-efficacy.

We might also aim to collect data for our Student Growth Objectives, or to organize our small groups for literacy instruction. Maybe we are seeking to buddy our students by high-low proficiency zones in order to encourage fluid conversation and allow for peer modeling. Or, as is often the case, we wish to track and give credit for growth in alternative areas related to successful integration that are not accounted for on a typical student grade report.

In any instance, one of the following quick tracking tools may be of immediate benefit. The thing is, we *know* that our Newcomer students show growth. Unfortunately, there's a pretty big jump from "Unsatisfactory" to "Partially Proficient" or from "Intermediate" to "Advanced" by way of standardized testing instruments. That can feel discouraging for us as teachers as well as for our students.

Our students deserve to understand that their gains are significant. We, as educators, deserve to know that our efforts are manifesting in student achievement. The following scales break the load of new information into more digestible pieces and allow for a fairer picture of Newcomer success.

Will these assessment measures be widely recognized as pieces of evidence? Don't bet on it. Will they help us to ensure that we are on the right track with our students? Will they help us to be inspired by how far our students have come? Will they guide us to be more purposeful in our instruction? Yes, yes, yes.

Newcomer Transition Markers

Student_____

Grade_____ Term_____

Observable	not met	approaching	met
Eye Contact			
Introductions, Hand shaking			
Co-ed Learning			
Sitting still for extended periods			
Sitting on carpet (if applicable)			
Walking in a line			
Participative learning			
Independent work			
Cooperative work			
Respect for others			
Homework			

Cultural Integration	not met	approaching	met
U.S. symbols recognition			
Major U.S. holidays			
Respond to basic directional cues			
Basic functional map use			
Basic geographical skill sets			
Basic calendar understanding			
Basic concepts of time			
Produce simple responses			
Ask essential questions			
Follow 3-step directions			
Report essential personal information			

© The Newcomer Fieldbook, 2017

School Integration

	not met	approaching	met
Safety rules and social norms			
School transportation efficacy			
Uniform/dress expectations			
School supply expectations			
Friend-making			
Lunch procedures			
Class changes and Locker use			
Computer use and policy			
Choice making			
Time management			
Personal hygiene			
Overall school engagement			

Stress & Trauma Indicators

	observed	not observed	referral
Speech Impediments			
Excessive sleepiness			
Reports of nightmares			
Routine physical pain			
Sensitivity to stimuli			
Frequent nausea			
Frequent nosebleeds			
Uncontrolled/frequent urination			
Uncontrolled/frequent bowel movements			
Compulsive behaviors			
Detachment			
Inability to maintain friendships			
Toe-walking, W-sitting			
Excessive disorganization			

Parent Participation	informed	uninformed	follow-up
Smoking/arms restrictions on campus			
Home and school discipline			
Health and vaccinations			
Student attendance expectations			
Parent-school participation			
Student homework			
Co-ed learning norms			
Student transportation			
Parent learning options			
School supply expectations			
Field trips			
Conferences			

Newcomer Academic Markers

Student_____

Grade_____ Term_____

Reading Readiness Level	1	2	3	4	5
Tracking (R-L)					
Page turning (R-L)					
Tracing					
Letter-sound recognition					
Upper and lower case differentiation					
Matching					
Sequencing					
Letter-sound phonemes					
Initial/end consonant identification					
Consonant blend identification					
Short and long vowel identification					
Diagraph identification					

Overall/Average Reading Readiness   _____

Reading Level	1	2	3	4	5
Sight words proficiency					
Onset and rhyme identification					
Decoding ability					
Reading proficiency					
Reading fluency					
Reading passage retell					
Sequence of events					
Predicting and Inferring					
Comparing and contrasting					

Summarizing					
Connections to text					
Overall text comprehension					

Overall/Average Reading   _____

Writing Level	1	2	3	4	5
Alphabet print proficiency					
Spacing					
Legibility					
Capital letters at beg. of sentences					
Basic conventions					
Intermediate/Advanced conventions					
Subject-verb agreement					
Sentence structure					
Paragraph structure					
Content					
Voice and Tone					

Overall/Average Writing   _____

Speaking Level	1	2	3	4	5
Introductions					
Yes/no responses					
Sentence fragments					
Express basic needs/commands					
Complete simple sentences					
Complete simple questions					

Speaking					
Use of familiar academic vocabulary					
Inflections (plurals, possessives, tense)					
Intonations					
Complete compound sentences					
Complete compound questions					
Use of advanced academic vocabulary					
Use of idioms, sarcasm, humor					

Overall/Average Speaking   _____

Listening	Level	1	2	3	4	5
Respond to simple commands						
Respond to simple questions						
Follow simple 3-step directions						
Retell 30sec-2min audio sequence						
Respond to compound commands						
Respond to compound questions						
Follow complex 3-step directions						
Retell 2min-5min audio sequence						
Respond to complex commands						
Respond to complex questions						
Follow 5-step directions						
Retell 5+min audio sequence						

Overall/Average Listening   _____

Overall/Average Combined   _____

© The Newcomer Fieldbook, 2017

REPORT CARDS FOR NEWCOMER ELLs

Translating student progress for our Newcomer-ESL students and their caregivers can be a complicated and daunting process, at best. Each district has their own means of processing report cards. Most use an online system, such as Infinite Campus. The same grading protocol and systems that apply to mainstream students will also apply to Newcomers. However, it may be necessary to take alternative approaches to sharing and clarifying students' achievements and concerns with parents.

The following Newcomer-friendly report card is a variation of a prototype created by a trusted colleague, Carmen Kuri. Carmen has extensive experience working with both refugee Newcomer and immigrant Spanish-speaking populations. In fact, Carmen herself is from Mexico. Her ELA-E teaching experience, combined with her personal background as an English Language Learner, allow Ms. Kuri a unique perspective on what parents and students need with regard to decoding typically complex report cards.

ELL abbreviated grade forms are not intended for use in place of traditional report cards. They are designed to accompany formal documents, which schools have a legal responsibility to provide to all families of enrolled students. Abbreviated forms do function well as a focal point for parent-teacher conferences. They may also be attached to formal report cards as an easy-to-digest summary.

Thanks for sharing, Ms. Kuri!

EL YAAFOURI

Language Modified Student Progress Report

Student Name_____ Date_____

Teacher_____ Grade_____

Subject	% Percentage	Not Meeting	Approaching	Meeting	Exceeding
Listening					
Speaking					
Reading					
Writing					
Math + − × ÷ =					
Science					
Social Studies					

Attendance					
Behavior					
Homework					

Comments:_____
_____
_____

Parent Signature_____ Teacher Signature_____

© The Newcomer Fieldbook, 2017

Section B: Assessment Accommodations for ELLs

Students who are designated as English Language Learners may be eligible for testing accommodations. Dr. Stephanie Cawthon, in the journal, *Practical Assessment, Research & Evaluation,* defines assessment accommodations as "a modification to the test that does not change validity or reliability of the test's results." The purpose of such additional supports during testing, she continues, is to "offer a student a better opportunity to demonstrate what he or she knows or can do."

The Educational Testing Service provides a similar description: "For ELLs, the primary goal of testing accommodations is to ensure that they have the same opportunity as students who have English as their first language to demonstrate their knowledge or skills in a content area." Of note, students who are assigned accommodations should not benefit from them such that they are set apart from students who are not allowed the same supports. Equity is the goal, all around.

Accommodations for ELLs are separate and distinct from those provided for special education students. This is because the special education accommodation assignment process is based on a student's IEP. The ELL equivalent of an IEP does not exist. Cawthon provides clarity: "Students with disabilities are eligible for a range of accommodations under the Individuals with Disabilities Education Improvement Act (IDEIA, 2004) and Section 504 of the Rehabilitation Act of 1973, as well as NCLB." Accommodations for non-native speakers are an allowance provided within the ELL designation.

In some cases, these arenas will overlap. This occurs when a child is at once designated as an ELL and determined to have special needs that would qualify him or her for an IEP and/or 504. An ELL *can* have an IEP as an autonomous allocation. This rarely occurs with Newcomers, because moves to recommend Newcomer students for special education testing and services are typically delayed for at least two years after arrival.

The delay in referring Newcomers for exceptional learner services is done to rule out language and adjustment complications that may cloud special education testing outcomes. Often, a Newcomer student who is eventually referred for special education services will have exceeded time limits for Newcomer programming by the time Response to Intervention (RTI) evaluations occur. Thus, he or she would be considered an ELL with an IEP or 504.

Currently, there are no formal state-to-state outlines as to what is considered optimal or acceptable with regard to testing accommodations for ELLs. Most major standardized test instruments, such as the PARCC, offer a prescribed set of allowed accommodations. However, individual schools and classrooms may provide separate or overlapping sets of accommodations for assessments within their immediate jurisdiction.

Let's take a look at a very general list of common testing accommodations for English Language Learners.

- Orally presented directions
- Orally presented questions in subjects other than reading
- Extended time to complete a test
- Extended time to complete class assignments that have assessment value
- Added breaks in testing periods or split testing blocks
- Small group testing
- Use of bilingual dictionaries
- Use of picture dictionaries
- Script or speech-to-text services
- Demonstrated exemplar (expectation of quality work)
- Direct translation of material
- Access to manipulatives (where applicable)
- Changes to the wording of direction and/or test questions
- Incorporation of visual supports and/or graphic organizer

A word of caution: accommodations are to be considered on an individual student basis, and are a direct reflection of a learner's specific needs and language accessibility level. The one-size-fits all approach is not effective, and may even be harmful. I can speak to this from experience.

In the early years of testing accommodations for Newcomers, I thought it would be reasonable to blanket my class with every available bit of aid for the state standardized test block. Let me be frank about all the ways that didn't work out. For my most advanced students, the accommodations, especially in the reading section, only served to slow students' reading and confuse the overall testing process. The supports did serve many of my intermediate students, while my most beginning English speakers made excellent play toys out of their picture dictionaries.

The extra time accommodation? Yes- I selected that one, too. As a class, we were finished in a quarter of the time… and then twiddled our fingers for the rest of the session, plus the extended time. Talk about wanting to pull your hair out.

Moral of the story: choose accommodations carefully and purposefully.

The intent of testing accommodations for language learners is to level the playing field, so to speak. This is done in two ways. First, accommodations should increase opportunities for all students to express knowledge and concept understanding by limiting the degree by which they are negatively impeded by mechanisms of language. Second, they should increase test score validity. Educational Testing Service (ETS) explains that "reducing or eliminating construct-irrelevant variance from the testing situation increases the likelihood that score users will be able to make the same valid interpretations of ELLs' scores as they make for other examinees."

If accommodations point away from these two key aims, skip them.

Considerations for testing supports should be the result of a team-based decision that is rooted in evidence around a student's demonstrated capacities. Bronwyn Coltrane of the Center for Applied Linguistics writes, "Accommodations should be selected carefully in order to ensure that ELLs are given appropriate support, including linguistic support, on standardized tests, especially when those tests are used as a basis for high-stakes decisions." This process of deliberating accommodations should consider the following:

- *What is the student's English proficiency level?*
- *What is known about his or her native language fluency level?*
- *Is the child familiar with standardized testing?*
- *How experienced is the student with specific accommodation tools?*
- *What supports will actually serve the student?*
- *Will certain supports prove erroneous, distracting or harmful in the testing setting?*
- *Will the selected accommodations increase a student's ability to demonstrate a truer extent of what he or she knows?*

Part of our role in working with language learners is to facilitate their ability to wholly participate in all parts of the school day, including periods of assessment. Accommodations are one means of facilitating this. Deliberate selection of accommodations, based on individual student data and classroom observations can enable us to more reliably gauge and monitor our students' deeper understanding of specific grade-appropriate content.

Select accommodations wisely, employ them only as long as needed, and take the time to celebrate each student's successes.

Section C: Transition, Program Exit and Re-designation

As students develop proficiency in the host language, they also progress along the language acquisition spectrum and make their way toward transitioning out of specified ELL services. Transition to exit is generally a multi-step process that allows for a gradual decrease in scaffolding and supports.

Re-designation occurs once the student is determined to have fully exited ELL programming and is no longer classified as an English Language Learner. WIDA clarifies re-designation in this way: "In general, English language learners (ELL) are no longer classified as limited-English proficient (LEP) once they have attained the language skills necessary to compete with mainstream English speakers in age and grade appropriate settings in all areas of language development without the use of adapted or modified English materials."

A series of initiatives must take place before re-designation can actually occur. In most cases, referrals for transition occur before any petition to exit ELL programming can be made. The transitional period is one in which a student conducts the majority of his or her learning in a traditional mainstream environment, but receives limited ongoing support in the area of language acquisition. Scaffolding techniques are moderated, and eventually cease, during the transitional phase.

Depending on school and district outlines, transition usually occurs when students reach the range of 3-5 on the WIDA ACCESS and/or WIDA "Can-Do" Indicators. Student progress during the transition phase is closely monitored. Under most state measures, ELLs can remain in transition for up to two years.

Exit is the final stage in the ELL re-designation process. As with progress monitoring, exit criteria is concurrent with state and district regulation and the language assessment instrument being used. Despite such localized input, ELL exit criteria is fairly consistent state-to-state.

For example, all efforts to reclassify a student must be grounded in a body of evidence and all cases must be carefully evaluated by a team of stakeholders, to include ELL and general education teachers, administrators, relevant school staff, and the student's parents or guardians. As part of the body of evidence, students must also demonstrate English language proficiency on one or more standardized assessments (e.g. a 4.5 minimum composite ACCESS score.)

Most ELL assessment frameworks caution against exiting students while they are still in the early grades. Generally, petitions for full program exit are not considered before the fourth grade. This is done to ensure that students have a solid foundation in both conversational and content-based academic English.

BODY OF EVIDENCE FILES FOR ELLs

Barbara Law and Mary Eckes elaborate on and organize a systematic framework called "The Quad", as originally conceptualized by Anthony, et al in 1992. "The Quad" provides and categorizes ideas about how to recognize and monitor student growth. The system is helpful in tracking ELLs and gathering evidence to support recommendations for movement out of language-intensive services.

The four divisions of Anthony's quadrant include: Observation of Process; Observation of Product; Classroom Measures; and Decontextualized Measures. The first two sections relate to formative assessment, while the latter speak to summative assessment.

As we work through a suggested Body of Evidence (BoE) checklist, we'll segment items into quadrant areas. Many of these particular suggestions come directly from Law and Eckes interpretation of "The Quad". Your individual school or district may require additional information. Take a few minutes to consider which quadrant each new data point will fall into. Ideally, we aim to achieve balance in completed student portfolios.

Oral assessments can be especially challenging. A reliable resource in this regard comes from Oregon State University. OSU's "Portfolio an Oral Examination Artifacts Checklist" can be located and printed at http://blogs.oregonstate.edu/matsecondaryhandbook/portfolio-and-oral-examination-artifacts-checklist/.

BoE files should be stored in a secure location and should follow the student as he or she moves through Newcomer level and/or grade level transitions. I really enjoy revisiting my students' BoEs. What a treat to see learning growth on such a tremendous scale.

TRANSITION & RE-DESIGNATION PROTOCOL

Newcomer transition occurs when a student demonstrates language proficiency to the extent that he or she is presumably equipped to meaningfully and successfully participate in a learning environment with fewer language supports. Thus, the individual is moved from one classroom and/or student cohort to another (for example: Newcomer Level 1 to Newcomer Level 2, Newcomer to Mainstream or High to Low Intervention). Re-designation occurs when a student demonstrates language proficiency to the extent that he or she no longer requires ELD services and is subsequently exited from English Language Development programming.

Both changes are contingent upon a sufficient body of evidence and stakeholder concurrence. Often, the student's teacher and the school's Instructional Services Advisory (ISA) team initially consider such determinations. If re-assignment seems like an appropriate action, additional stakeholders are consulted. Such individuals may include Newcomer teacher(s), mainstream teacher(s), parents, administrators, and site-based ELD specialists.

If the student meets criteria for transition/re-designation, and if stakeholders agree that classroom re-assignment and/or a full program exit is in the best interest of the learner, the changeover is set in motion. It is typically beneficial for a student to visit and spend time in the new classroom setting before fully transitioning. For example, a Newcomer student who is eligible for re-assignment might spend only the math period in a mainstream class for several weeks prior to a complete roster change. Gradual passage can ease some of the anxiety that comes with novelty- and which may be exacerbated for many Newcomers.

A sample documents for ELD exit communication is included on the following page. Depending on your specific school and district, ELD may need to be replaced with ESL or a separate classification.

Recommended Body of Evidence (BoE) Checklist for ELLs

Standardized Forms
- ☐ Cover page
- ☐ Included Contents
- ☐ Student data, including prior school records and medical information
- ☐ Heritage Language Survey data
- ☐ Student placement data
- ☐ Parent Contact Log
- ☐ Behavioral intervention information

Observation of Process:
- ☐ Notes on evidence toward proficiency in:
  Speaking, Listening, Reading, Writing

Observation of Product
- ☐ Student work samples
  - Reading logs
  - Writing journals/writing samples
  - Small group journals/peer evaluations
  - Self-evaluations, Peer-evaluations
  - Thematic projects, Portfolios
  - Student audio/video recordings
  - Homework
  - Selected work samples from previous grades, if applicable

Classroom Measures
- ☐ Classroom-based assessments
  - Spelling assessments
  - Running records
  - Exit tickets
  - Skills inventories
  - Sight-words inventories
- ☐ Curriculum-based assessments
  - End of unit tests
  - Comprehension assessments
  - Reading Level diagnostics

Decontextualized Measures
- ☐ Standardized/formal assessment measures
  - ACCESS assessment data
  - District Testing data
  - State Testing Data (PARCC, etc.)
  - Computerized assessment data (STARR, iReady, etc.)
  - Report Cards/Parent-Teacher Conference Reports

Notice of ELD Program Exit

The _____ School District is pleased to inform you that your child is approved to exit the English Language Development (ELD) program.

A number of criteria are used to determine if a student is prepared to exit ELD services. We are pleased to inform you that based on student work samples, teacher input and standardized test scores, your child no longer requires specialized ELD instruction.

Your child, _____ is ready to **exit the English Language Development (ELD) program** at _____ school, as demonstrated by a body of evidence that includes a language assessment score of _____.

The purpose of ELD programming is to ensure English language proficiency for non-English speakers. The program explicitly teaches students listening, speaking, reading and writing skills. Once students exit from ELD programming, they no longer receive:

- Standardized testing accommodations for ELLs (English Language Learners).
- Extra time to complete assignments
- Specialized ELD pull-out or push-in services
- Use of bilingual dictionaries during testing
- Required scaffolded instruction services

Unless otherwise notified, your child will be exited from ELD programming, effective _____/_____/_____.

If you have questions or concerns, please contact your child's school or teacher directly.

I have read and understand this statement and/or this statement has been read or translated for me, and I understand its contents.

Name _____ Signature_____

Date _____ Translator_____

© The Newcomer Fieldbook, 2017

CONTINUED MONITORING

According to federal Title III legislation, all exited ELLs must continue to be monitored for a full two years after the re-designation has been finalized. The Area Education Agency explains that the purpose of continued evaluation is "to ensure success and a rapid response should the student begin to struggle."

Note: As previously noted, schools have a legal obligation to inform parents of a child's eligibility for ELD services. A similar legal stipulation ensures that parents receive written notification from the school of the child's reclassification status.

A sample documents for ELD exit communication is included on the following page. Depending on your specific school and district, ELD may need to be replaced with ESL or a separate classification.

ADDITIONAL RESOURCES:

EduSkills (paid service): eduskills.com

Speaking/listening tracking sheets:
http://www.learnalberta.ca/content/eslapb/trackingsheets.html

Tracking Progress for ELLs:
http://journals.sagepub.com/doi/pdf/10.1177/003172170909100306

WIDA Rubrics for ELLs: http://wida.us

U.S. Department of Education: Tools and Resources for Monitoring and Exiting English Learners from EL Programs and Services
https://www2.ed.gov/about/offices/list/oela/english-learner-toolkit/chap8.pdf

Mrs. Corpuz's ESL World: Data Tracking
http://mscorpuz.weebly.com/data-tracking.html

Mrs. Castro's Class: WIDA Progress Monitoring Spreadsheet
http://mrscastrospanglishstyle.blogspot.com/2012/04/wida-can-do-classroom-templatefreebie.html

7 FAMILY RESOURCE & WELCOME CENTERS

> **Guiding Questions for Chapter 7:**
> -- What is our clarified vision around Newcomer family and parent support?
> -- Does a welcome center factor into that vision for us? Does it make sense based on our needs, goals and demographics?
> -- If so, what does that look like in the present tense? In the immediate future? The long-term future?
> -- What kinds of human resources are (or could be) available that would enable parent and family support for Newcomer families?
> -- How do we fully recognize and employ the assets of the people on our team and maximize the value of our professional network?
> -- We don't need to reinvent the wheel. Who or what organizations can we visit, read about, speak to and learn from?
> -- How will we measure the effectiveness of our efforts?

Strengthening the School-Home Connection

Call it what you will- Family Welcome Center, Family Resource Center, Community Outreach Center, or Newcomer Orientation Center. For each name variation, the underlying structural intention is the same. For ease of understanding, we'll refer to these programs in total as "welcome centers". In any regard, welcome centers can be an exceptional asset to any school-based Newcomer initiative. The U.S. Department of Education writes this:

"Schools may need to explicitly reach out to Newcomer-ESL families and request that they participate in two-way communication, and collaborate with teachers and school leaders, to support their child's learning and development. Newcomer-ESL families need to know that their voices count, and they need to learn how to be heard in the school. The school can link parents to adult education opportunities as well as social and cultural resources."

Welcome centers achieve these precise aims. As previously mentioned in *The Newcomer Student*, welcome centers vary significantly in terms of aesthetics, structure, and range of offerings, based on site specifics and serviceable clients. Some centers are imbedded in the operation of an individual campus; others are district-wide initiatives with extensive outreach. There is no *right* or *wrong*. There is only *existing* or *not existing*. Strive to achieve and improve upon the former.

WHERE TO BEGIN?

The U.S. Department of Education recommends that the following "Core Components" be considered when planning, constructing and improving parent involvement efforts for Newcomer families: a) Academic Success; b) Advocacy and Decision-Making; and c) Awareness and Use of Resources. Each area that we will explore falls into one of these categories.

Academic Success efforts relate to informing and including parents about how their child will engage in school and how they can best aid their child's academic and social success. The *Advocacy and Decision-Making* component aims to strengthen caregivers' understanding of their rights in advocating for and actively participating in school-based decisions that impact their child. *Awareness and use of Resources* refers to the process of purposefully and consistently alerting families to school-based and community-based resources that could be of benefit.

The services that you choose to offer at your school and/or site welcome center will be a reflection of your program goals, population needs and available funding. If you are contemplating your potential range of services, here are a few thoughts to consider!

SCHOOL-BASED HELP

Welcome Centers should, above all else, serve as an essential link between Newcomer families and the school itself. Such services may include: translation of school fliers, coordinating teacher conferences, explanation of school rules, uniform purchase assistance, communicating a child's medical needs, or organizing parent volunteer opportunities.

MENTAL HEALTH COUNSELING SERVICES

Counseling services, or at least an explicit acknowledgement of opportunities to participate in counseling, may be part of the orientation process. In some instances, counseling services are provided at a child's school. In other scenarios, a school may fulfill this need via community partnerships. It is expected that school-based counselors and psychologists who work with diverse populations are adequately trained and prepared to meet the unique needs of Newcomer students.

Parents and adult caretakers do not have access to the same counseling and therapy services that their children may receive during the school day. However, alternative services for adults may be made available through the welcome center. In any event, guardians of Newcomer students should be presented with information on how to access counseling services as part of the orientation process.

PHYSICAL HEALTH SERVICES

Health services accessibility requires similar attention as an element of Newcomer orientation.

What services are families eligible for? How do they enroll in and/or monitor coverage? What is the difference between a doctor's office and hospital visit? Where are these resources located? How do referrals work? What specific immunizations are required for school enrollment? How much do services cost?

These items may be detailed in a simple pamphlet, posted in a Family Resource area, or directly discussed with a family. Additionally, many schools offer students access to a part-time nurse. Some school complexes offer basic sports physicals or immunization services on-site. This information should be included in the orientation tool kit.

Health literacy is an important feature of physical health servicing and provides explicit direction with regard to self-care. Topics may include: nutrition, disease prevention, hygiene, oral care, stress management, depression, and vitamin care.

PUBLIC BENEFITS & COMMUNITY RESOURCES

Immigrant and Newcomer families may be eligible for a range of services that serve the purpose of aiding transition and resettlement. Often, families are not aware that certain (or any) services exist.

Does the family qualify for financial assistance? Food assistance? Transportation vouchers? Are family members aware of low-cost clothes purchase options? Job training? Translation services? What adult ESL classes, technical training or technology courses could benefit the family? What are the options for free or low-cost childcare for working caretakers? Newcomer centers act as reliable clearinghouses for such information. Be sure to make these options clear and readily accessible!

CAREER COUNSELING SERVICES

I love this idea from San Francisco's Newcomer High School, which offers an Inter-district Cultural Exchange program. The purpose of this program is to "bring together students from Newcomer High with mainstream students from other schools in the district." As part of the exchange, students attend and participate in cultural events and engage in one another's school and living communities.

PARENT ENGAGEMENT EXPECTATIONS

Making sure that their children go to school each day is the most important thing that parents and caretakers can do for their learners in the host setting. Adults can also help young learners succeed by ensuring that their children are completing homework, are getting enough sleep at night and come to school in uniform and have a quiet space to work at home, among other things. Newcomer parents are eager to support their students' school endeavors. In many cases, this simply requires a clear explanation as to how, when and why parent involvement at a child's school occurs in the host setting.

COMMUNITY ORIENTATION

Our incoming families are eager to engage in their new communities in healthy, productive, law-abiding ways. What does that look like, exactly? Our adult Newcomers may require explicit training regarding culturally normative behaviors and citizenry expectations in the new setting.

What are the essential symbols of the new country and state? What are the meanings behind popular icons? What specific laws relate to community participation? Parenting and discipline? Alcohol and substance use? Obtaining a driver's license? How are families expected to participate in their neighborhoods? What is expected with regard to workplace behavior? What major holidays are observed in the new country? What actions are anticipated when meeting someone for the first time?

Such information may be presented in a class setting. It may be offered as a module or booklet. If such services are not offered at the school, where can adults be directed to in order to engage in similar coursework?

FAMILY-COMMUNITY PARTNERSHIPS

Just as incoming students can benefit from a school "buddy" to show them the ropes and introduce them to peers, the same processes can help families as they resettle into new areas. Families who are already living in a local neighborhood may sign up through the school or welcome center to host or buddy a Newcomer family. Host families might help incoming families learn where the nearest grocery store is located or how to use a public library. They may introduce them to other neighbors or plan to attend key school events together. Often, these partnerships lead to long lasting friendships between families!

CITIZENSHIP COURSEWORK

Citizenship coursework can help alert adults to the important rights and responsibilities they have as individuals living in the United States of America. Adults who wish to become (or are already in the process of becoming) U.S. citizens may receive additional support in preparing for their naturalization interview, civics text and English test.

CREDIT AND FINANCIAL COUNSELING

Adults who are new to the United States may require explicit direction with regard to banking, finances and credit counseling. This can occur as a component of orientation programming, adult citizenship coursework or as a separate effort within the local community.

How do U.S. banks operate? How do I open an account? What is a credit score? How is it calculated and managed? What are the advantages and disadvantages of obtaining a credit card? How are utilities calculated, and how do I pay them? How do I participate in online bill pay? What happens if my payment is late or if my account is compromised? What if I cannot pay my bills?

LEGAL AND IMMIGRATION SERVICES

The U.S. immigration process is a thorough one, full of twists and turns that are capable of disorienting the best of us. Imagine navigating this process as a non-English speaker. To compound matters, more than a few sharks are waiting to take advantage of Newcomers as they engage in this process. Often, refugee and immigrant families will pay for "legal" services that are not rendered, incomplete, or shoddily performed.

Thus, a key goal of any Family Resource Center should be to provide access to legitimate legal help for ESL families. California's Zellerbach Family Foundation has made a vocal commitment to "increase access to reliable and affordable immigration legal services and decrease fraudulent immigration practices." If such services are not available on or near your campus, it may be helpful to point families in the right direction of such resources as part of the orientation program.

In addition to immigration policy, families may require legal counsel in the areas of labor and employment, family matters, housing issues, health care related concerns, or credit/financial disputes.

ADULT ESL and HIGH SCHOOL DEGREE EQUIVALENT TEST PREPARATION

Many resources exist on the topic of adult ESL, and this is not my area of expertise. However, the following document is useful with regard to adult participation. It is a reflection of the Heritage Language Survey for students, with queries that are more relevant in getting to know your adult Newcomer populations. The same considerations and notes that apply to the student version hold true. Namely, the contents of the adult participation documents cannot be used for the purpose of determining or contesting and individual's legal status.

VOLUNTEER REGISTRATION

A sample form is included after the Adult ESL Heritage Survey.

THE NEWCOMER FIELDBOOK

Adult ESL Heritage Survey

_____

SCHOOL/CAMPUS

Participant _____ Translator _____

Phone Number _____ Email _____

DISCLAIMER: All information is used for the sole purpose of identifying client needs and recommending relevant programming. Responses **cannot** be used to:

✖ Determine or question immigration status

✖ Contest students and/or family members in legal matters

Language Data

What is your country of origination? _____

Secondary countries? _____

What is your first language?

☐ English ☐ Spanish ☐ Other _____

What language is usually spoken in your home?

☐ English ☐ Spanish ☐ Other _____

How long have you been learning English?   Years _____ Months _____

How would you like to receive information from the school (when possible)?

☐ In English   ☐ In Spanish

☐ In another language _____

© The Newcomer Fieldbook, 2017

I have children at home:
☐ YES _____ ☐ NO

I currently have children enrolled in U.S. schools:
☐ YES _____ ☐ NO

Someone is our home drives a car: ☐ YES   ☐ NO
I am currently employed:
☐ YES   where? _____ ☐ NO

I have completed formal schooling to level:
☐ elementary school (U.S. grades kindergarten-5th grade)
☐ middle school (U.S. grades 6th-8th grade)
☐ high school (U.S. grades 9th-12th grade)   ☐ some college
☐ Bachelor's degree _____ ☐ Advanced_____

I have work experience in the following areas:
Work place/Type of work   *How long?*
_____   _____
_____   _____
_____   _____
_____   _____

I would rate my current English language abilities as:
☐ I do not know any English   ☐ I know a little bit of English   ☐ I can understand basic English, but I do not speak it much   ☐ I can understand and speak some basic English   ☐ I understand a lot of English and feel somewhat confident speaking it   ☐ I feel very confident in my English abilities
☐ OR, on a scale:
1   2   3   4   5   6   7   8   9   10

By participating in Adult ESL classes, I hope to improve:
☐ basic communication   ☐ advanced language skills   ☐ work-place communication   ☐ my ability to become employed   ☐ my ability to help my child in school   ☐ my ability to get a driver's license   ☐ my ability to return to school/college   ☐ other _____

Family Resource Center Volunteer Registration

Thank you for your interest in volunteering! Please return completed applications to:

_____

First Name:	
Last Name:	
Street Address:	
City: State: Zip Code:	
First Language:	
Second Language(s):	

Volunteer skills: ☐ mentorship   ☐ organization   ☐ driving   ☐ translation

☐ heavy lifting   ☐ fundraising/grant writing   ☐ event planning   ☐ clerical

☐ computer skills   ☐ marketing   ☐ other_____

Areas of professional/scholastic expertise:

Areas of interest:

Availability: ☐ Mon ☐ Tues ☐ Wed ☐ Thurs ☐ Fri ☐ Sat ☐ Sun

☐ Morning   ☐ Afternoons   ☐ Evenings

ADDITIONAL INFORMATION

_____
_____
_____
_____

© The Newcomer Fieldbook, 2017

Next Steps

We've explored most of the components of welcome center servicing. Now it's time to apply them to your organization's unique circumstance. What will your plan be?

Not all elements will make sense to implement at your location. What resources does your team have? The facilities for? What knowledge and expertise? What items could be integrated in the future, with proactive planning? What are you currently doing that could be expanded?

Are there resources in your community that already provide some of these services? Are you prepared to direct families to these locations? Do you already have established working relationships between your team and support organizations? How can those ties be strengthened?

Take a few moments to brainstorm these thoughts. Then, work toward your mission and vision (or revisit your existing statements) to check for clarity and defined purpose.

Newcomer Family Resource Center Framework

The mission and vision for the _____ Center is as follows:

Mission:_____
_____
_____
_____

Vision:_____
_____
_____
_____

8 WORKING THROUGH CULTURE & BIAS

> Guiding Questions for Chapter 8:
> -- Do we create and maintain a place of safety and comfort where professionals can take risks in sharing personal thoughts?
> -- Can we be honest with ourselves about our unique sets of biases? Can we be successful in encouraging our teammates to do the same?
> -- How will evaluation of educator biases in our building positively or negatively impact our students?
> -- How do or can we capture baseline data regarding the true state of our school or classroom culture?
> -- What steps do we agree to take that will enhance positive culture in our building?
> -- How will we monitor our growth and success in these endeavors?

Culture & Diversity Awareness Training

Learners with refugee and immigrant backgrounds are highly likely to endure cultural disorientation as part of the transition to living and attending school in the host country. Newcomer students are statistically more prone to teacher-learner disconnect and incidents of bullying. They are also likely to experience a diminished ability to self-advocate as well as both real and perceived difficulties "fitting in".

While it is essential that Newcomers become familiar with the rules, customs, language and expectations of the dominant host culture, it is equally imperative that cultural awareness- if not outright tolerance- is explicitly taught and modeled in host school settings.

Cultural understanding is indispensable within schools, especially in the context of incompatible norms around "appropriate" demonstrations of positive student participation. Misevaluations by teachers of student behavior and intent are frequent in classrooms where Newcomer students are present. If left unattended, these misperceptions fester and become "truths" that can be used to negatively stereotype a specific population or vast cultural groups.

Meanwhile, youth have a strong tendency to mimic adult behavior and feeling patterns. If teacher-modeled behaviors contain unhealthy biases, students will absorb these tendencies. When this occurs, it becomes very difficult for a healthy classroom climate to exist. Detrimental bias patterns can expand to negatively impact the climate and culture of a school.

Cultural norms are those having to do with social, religious, familial, linguistic, and artistic values of a nation or its peoples. Often, these values are implicitly taught through exposure and become imbedded features of an individual's unique composite. Value structures are not always overt. Often, they are only revealed when an opposing value system is introduced, bringing known expectations into question.

Values can fluctuate. New norms can be learned, or even live in duplicity with the old ones.

Refugee Newcomer students face the challenge of navigating the abrupt interchange of vastly different normative value systems in the process of resettlement. Educators may also be challenged to support Newcomer students in their classrooms and to overcome personal biases surrounding new populations. Thus, the role of schools must expand to accommodate these unconventional learning needs, on the part of both the incoming student and the host faculty.

CULTURAL MISALIGNMENTS AT SCHOOL

Cultural norms and values, even if disseminated by particular region, religion or family, are virtually limitless. Only the most prevalent and pressing observations will be addressed here. In exploring heritage-to-host culture misalignments, the most pressing issues include norms around eye contact, left-handedness, "saving face" ideology, parent involvement and concepts of time.

Direct eye contact with an adult or elder, in many cultures, is considered a demonstration of intense disrespect. Meanwhile, a diverted gaze is considered the utmost sign of esteem. In these contexts, parents explicitly teach children to look down or away from the face of authority figures, including teachers. Here, the cultural expectations between the heritage and host countries are not aligned. Providing Newcomer students and their families with explicit clarification around eye contact norms, for example, invites new families to explore new ways of thinking and behaving that facilitate comprehensive integration.

In many cultures, the left hand is considered "unclean". The virtuous right hand should be used for all socially observed activities: eating, sharing or passing items, receiving gifts, and writing. When working with Newcomer parents, it is wise to practice awareness in delivering or receiving papers or other items. In working with children, the issue of left-handedness may present itself. A child who naturally presents as left-handed may be intensely discouraged from the behavior at home. Students and parents of left-handed children may require permission (or candid encouragement) to exercise left-handedness in the school capacity.

"Saving Face" refers to a societal notion that an individual operates as an inherently connected part of the larger family and community organism. In this way, each small act by an individual within the family has larger implications for the reputation of the group as a whole, or on the family name. In the classroom setting, students with strong "saving face" values may hesitate to participate or volunteer for fear of failure resulting in real or perceived disgracing of the family reputation. Students whose cultures are structured around "saving face" principles benefit from co-operative talk structures (over individual call-outs) and safe, structured classroom climates.

Parent involvement expectations vary greatly across countries and cultures. The Western model, which assumes parents' active participation in students' school endeavors, is an unfamiliar archetype for much of the world's population. In many regions, overt parent involvement in academic functions is considered rude and imposing. In this way, educators are considered authorities in all aspects of learning; parents honor the teacher in this role, and trust the teacher to make key decisions surrounding their child's learning success.

Out of respect, family members defer such responsibilities to academic personnel and refrain from school activism. Many Newcomer parents require a straightforward introduction to Western norms for parent involvement at school. Most respond positively to such guidance, and many thrive when they are introduced to (and given safe opportunities to) function *within* the school community.

The importance of time fluctuates regionally. In many areas, adherence to time is not strictly valued and is overshadowed by interpersonal connection. In many cultures, it is inappropriate to refuse an opportunity to participate in conversation with a fellow community member. Thus, a 9:00 appointment may be realized at 11:00 or noon; and it is not usually considered rude to arrive later than indicated, unless clearly specified in advance. Parents and students in Western host regions may benefit from direct explanation of the importance of time in our culture. Students gain from set schedules, positive reinforcement for timeliness and adult modeling of the expected behavior.

When I lived in Tanzania, for example, a twenty-minute walk to our school might be a three-hour adventure. I might, along the path, encounter a friend. If the friend wished to talk for long periods, or invite me for tea, it would have been all but impossible for me to shoo off the gesture in a rushed tone, as we commonly do here in the States. After tea, I might come upon a stranger. After a quick introduction, she might inform me that she needs help carrying goods from the market to her home. It would be expected for me to accompany her both to the market and to her house.

A phone call to work to explain my tardiness would not have been necessary, unless we had a pressing engagement that day. In arranging important affairs in Tanzania, we'd make an important distinction: *Are we talking African time or American time?* This is not an offensive query. It is a clarifying one. Time moves slower in many countries than it does in ours. Neither context is superior, but an awareness of the difference can reduce confusion and frustration.

Cultural variances that are so wholly unusual to one party or another often require frank explanation. As the second prong to success, schools have an obligation to work through judgments related to cultural differences. We accomplish this by providing opportunities to practice new thought patterns and adjust social interactions in a safe context. Incoming Newcomer students should receive appropriate and ongoing orientation to host cultural norms. In the same way, teachers and students in the host setting can benefit immensely from explicit awareness of globally diverse cultural norms.

Culture & Bias

Humans have an incredible capacity to instantly process information about other humans, and then make rapid judgments based on that information. This is in our nature, and it is nature's way of protecting us. We sometimes call it *gut*, *instinct* or *intuition*. However, rapid judgment can be harmful if and when they evolve into biases, especially when biases begin to dictate our general perception of other humans.

Our brains take in critical new information via one of two processing channels. One involves unconscious thought, while the other is ruled by conscious evaluation and response. Unconscious thought is automatized and usually emotionally driven. Conscious thought is reflective and controlled.

When we meet new people or begin to establish new relationships, our brains respond with a flurry of conscious and unconscious activity. We are analyzing the other individual and making a series of analyses based on the stimulation that our brain is receiving. We are producing and activating biases.

Prejudices, stereotypes and discriminatory evaluations are unconscious thinking patterns. Often, these thought-processing channels were constructed in our early childhood, influenced by our role models, societal constructs and media. Reinforced or repeated prejudices eventually become automatic. They become ingrained information-processing mechanisms.

EXPLORING PERSONAL BIASES

Let's be honest. We all have biases. Some are large, some small. Certain prejudices negatively impact our interactions with others, or even our work. What draws us together is that we all have them. There can be no throwing stones, here. We are all peering at each other from glass houses, our little (and big) biases tucked away in drawers and cabinets and crawl spaces. From a more scientific standpoint,

> "As we are repeatedly exposed to stereotypical associations and prejudices from an early age, these become automated in our long-term memory. At the same time, the outward expression of internalized bias is curbed by strong social norms and legal restrictions against expressed prejudice and discrimination. The result is a subtle, hidden, and often unconscious negative bias towards particular social groups. *Even individuals who truly believe they are non-prejudiced hold unconscious bias.*"   (Culture Plus, 2015)

So, it's out on the table. I have prejudices. You have prejudices. Our students and their parents carry biases into the school each day. Some of those are friendly, harmless judgments. Many are not.

We have a responsibility to mitigate our own biases to whatever extent we are able. This duty carries remarkable weight, based on the nature of our work with children and the inevitable part we play as role models in urban, multicultural settings. It is also our task to encourage a shift in the negative biases that exist in our parents and students, Newcomer and non-Newcomer alike.

DOING THE WORK

The question. It comes up, right on cue, every single time. *Why? Why do we want to get in there, so close to our own (and other's) vulnerabilities?*

These aren't exactly our finest hours and shiniest strengths we're digging up here. In fact, the whole thing is a very uncomfortable exercise in opening seemingly unnecessary cans of worms. Not exactly the way the ideal way to spend professional development time today. Right?

I'll tell you why.

Because evidence strongly indicates that unconscious biases can be overcome, and even reversed, with sincere intent. In fact, "A person who is motivated to be unprejudiced—because of legal sanctions, social pressures, or strong personal egalitarian values—can suppress biased responses." (Culture Plus)

In a fascinating turn of events, the human mind is capable of overriding itself. We are capable of re-imagining our vision of the world around us.

In order for true culture and bias training to be effective, we have to make way for it to *be* effective. That process begins with us taking the time to be raw and honest with ourselves about our own apparent and underlying prejudices. There's no promise that the process will be pretty, or even particularly enjoyable. However, be assured that by taking the first steps in being truthful with ourselves, we can open doors for growth and improvement, both in our lives and in the the lives of the students we serve.

The most impactful culture and bias workshops encourage and enhance the self-exploratory process. In a school-wide or organizational setting, professional development may occur in whole group or small group contexts. Ultimately, open discussion around individual biases tends to embolden healthy whole-group conversation around campus-wide bias concerns. When educators model behaviors associated with the shedding of unhealthy biases, they empower students to do the same. This is the most durable means of strengthening school culture and removing unnecessary obstructions to academic and social achievement.

Workshop Introduction

The Culture & Bias Workshop form is designed to begin this self-exploratory process. For now, start here. Remember- this doesn't need to be shared with anyone. However, if you're seeking a bolder move with bigger payoffs for our students, then I certainly recommend embarking on the endeavor of highlighting honest biases as a school-wide initiative. Opening these doors, uncomfortable as it may be at first, creates room for honest conversation in a safe, structured environment- and aligns with a path toward true and lasting impact.

Culture and Bias Workshop

To me, diversity means:
_____
_____

To me, culture means:
_____
_____

If I had to define myself by 3 standard social-construct categories, I would be:

_____, _____, _____

If I designed my own social categories, I would define myself as:

_____, _____, _____

How do I describe the type of environment was I raised in?
_____
_____

In what ways did my experiences as a child impact my world-view as an adult?
_____
_____

What comes to mind when I think about my interactions with adult authority figures?
_____
_____

How did those experiences shape similar interactions in later parts of my life?
_____
_____

On a scale of 1 to 10, how do I rate my level of comfort in interacting with diverse populations ------?

As a very young child	1 2 3 4 5 6 7 8 9 10
As an older child	1 2 3 4 5 6 7 8 9 10
As a teen	1 2 3 4 5 6 7 8 9 10
As a young adult	1 2 3 4 5 6 7 8 9 10
As an experienced adult	1 2 3 4 5 6 7 8 9 10

What I notice about these ratings is:

_____

_____

_____

_____

I think that might be because:

_____

_____

_____

_____

My most comfortable experience with diversity was:

_____

_____

My most vulnerable or challenging experience with diversity was:

_____

_____

On a scale of 1 to 10, how diverse is my immediate friendship circle?
1 2 3 4 5 6 7 8 9 10

On a scale of 1 to 10, how diverse is my work/colleague circle?
1 2 3 4 5 6 7 8 9 10

On a scale of 1 to 10, how diverse is my student population?
1 2 3 4 5 6 7 8 9 10

I feel most natural teaching students who:

_____

_____

I feel most awkward or underprepared in working with students who:

_____

_____

Humans have biases. I am human and I have biases! My outright biases are:

_____

_____

_____

I am not comfortable sharing all of my biases publicly. A personal bias I know for myself to be true is: ------------------------. *Don't panic!* ☺ *Use this as thinking time only.*

Some biases are detrimental. With regard to my thinking around culture and diversity, I believe that I can grow in the area(s) of:

_____

_____

_____

_____

Classroom "Agreements"

School-based expectations are a traditional component of classroom management and imperative to the Newcomer framework. Before we go any further, however, I'd like to invite you to gently sidestep away from the idea of "rules" (if you haven't done so already). Personally, when I think of this word, I also think of rigidity and limitations. Our hope for our students is not that they are limited in their capacity, but that they know how to appropriately channel that capacity in positive, productive ways.

I choose to refer to classroom rules as "Classroom Agreements" or even "Choice Opportunities". These tool sets define optimal social behavior patterns that serve the greater good and function of a shared working or learning space. The goal of shared social structures at school is to engage students in understanding and practicing positive behaviors, while together creating a safe, healthy place for learning.

In this way, students are capable of *choosing* to support the community good. They can agree (or disagree) to participate in healthy ways. This stimulates a perspective shift from "don't" (rule structure) to "do" (agreement structure). We want our students to be *doers*, right?

Classroom agreements are important in all classroom settings, but are invaluable in the Newcomer setting. They create routine, structure and predictability- the backbones of safety- while encouraging social behaviors that are accepted as normative in the host environment.

Students, especially those who may be coming from a different school, state or country, adjust their social cues (or learn new ones) by observing others in their new environment. Classroom agreements provide predictable paths toward desired social outcomes. All the while, by agreeing to act in ways that support whole-class learning, students are actively building and being part of a community. As students find safety in explicit routines (many of which ultimately become implicit habits), other energies, such as distress and concern, can be redirected toward the key objective at hand, which is *learning*.

HOW DO I CREATE CLASSROOM AGREEMENTS?

The most effective way to create Classroom Agreements is to take the "I" out of it altogether. This should be a team process and effort. Part of building trust is making room for students' input.

Working agreements are a great way to begin a year or a new course. Invite students to envision a class environment that is safe, happy and productive. Collaborate with students to create clear, simple statements about behaviors that reflect the nature of that picture. If expressiveness in the host language is a challenge here, a "Looks Like/Sounds Like/Feels Like" chart can be a great way to go.

One recommendation: aim to create agreement statements that are broad-based. This strategy limits the number of agreements necessary for students to recall and also reinforces the idea that agreements are normative behaviors that respect the safety and well-being of the entire group. For example, "We come to class prepared and ready to learn." might envelop a myriad of smaller 'rules': *Turn in your homework; No chewing gum; No cell phones*. "We are respectful and kind to one another" embodies ideas such as: *share with others; raise your hand to speak; no pushing*.

For Newcomers, broad-based agreements may require additional instruction that intentionally focuses on cultural norms in the host setting. For example, if we look at our above examples, "We come to class prepared and ready to learn." could also encompass: *We are dressed appropriately for school and for the weather. We bring a pencil to school (or know where to locate one at school). We ask for help when we need it. We try to stay on topic when we are talking with partners about our learning.*

The second example, "We are respectful and kind to one another." will likely involve a detour into these areas: *shake hands when greeting; observe expected bodily proximity; use appropriate volume within a given context; acknowledge both male and female classmates; establish eye contact with adults; hold the door for others; separate tribal differences from school interactions.*

Of course, each of these broader agreements will require discussion- great! Have students draw and label their thoughts, create a mural expressing these aims, act out ideal (and not ideal) behaviors or actions, or write/draw/label a story about how someone acted toward them demonstrating (or not demonstrating) attributes of the class' agreements. Again, "Looks Like..." charts are really helpful in this regard.

Refer to your agreements regularly. Praise and reinforce positive behaviors. Follow through with consequences for not-so-positive choice making (engage students in designing these consequences, too!). Show your own commitment to your "Class Agreements" by walking the walk. Remember, so much of what your students learn about healthy behaviors, social norms and cultural biases, they will learn just by observing you. Make *your* words and actions count.

Note: Classroom Agreements are most effective when they work in tandem with school agreements. It is highly recommended that agreements are implemented and valued as a building-wide initiative. This process creates a common foundation upon which community, tolerance and learning can flourish.

Cultivating School-Based Culture

Culture. It's the latest education buzzword to catch fire, and it is applied to a seemingly endless range of affairs. We refer to our students' heritage cultures. We toss around the idea of a school culture, a classroom culture, a staff culture. So, what *exactly* are we talking about here? In the simplest possible terms, we can look at it in this way:

"Culture is the way you think, act and interact." –Anonymous

From this lens, it is indeed possible to reference "culture" across such a variety of social platforms. How our students think, act and interact at home and in their communities is a reflection of their heritage culture. How we think, act and interact at work is a reflection of our work culture.

Let's consider our schools and classrooms from this same vantage. Looking to the best versions of ourselves and our programs, what do we envision as an optimal learning culture for our students and staff? How are we encouraged to think, act and interact with our students and colleagues? How are we teaching learners to engage with each other in affirmative ways?

As a school or classroom leader, these are important thoughts to map out. My ideas may not look the same as your ideas. That's ok. We can lay some common ground, though. The following cues present an opportunity to check in with your own vision of school culture. How can you help to improve the way that your team thinks, acts and interacts?

8 Ways to Optimize a Learning Culture

1. Invest in Students:
We all ache to know that someone we care about is standing firmly behind or beside us. If our aim is to increase a student's success rate, our honest investment in both their present capacity and future potential is non-negotiable. Express a genuine interest in each individual. Learn how to pronounce student's names correctly and begin using them on the very first day. Ask questions about students' heritage culture and allow for safe opportunities to share these insights with other classmates. Offer relevant multicultural reading materials. Post flags or maps, and have students mark their heritage country. Be a listener. Find out what students find interesting. Commit to supporting students with time-in over time-out. Show up. Keep promises. Practice being present and mindful with students. Nurture connectivity.

2. Provide Choice:
When presented with choice-making opportunities in a safe, predictable environment, learners develop self-efficacy and strategizing abilities. We can scaffold these processes to enable students to grow as wise decision makers. Begin by limiting the range of available options. Model reasoning through active think-alouds. Also, it is important to allow time for students to consider and process potential gains and sacrifices involved when choosing between items or activities. Similarly, prompt students to predict the probable consequences of unwise choice making and to reflect on these outcomes when they occur. Incorporate choice making throughout the day. Station (center) activities, choice of paper color, homework, reading book, order of task completion and game selection are manageable places to start. When students are invited to make healthy choices- and have opportunities to practice doing so- they are much more inclined to become invested, engaged learners.

3. Provide Clarity:
Students, not unlike adults, desire to know what is expected of them. Who doesn't enjoy a road map to success? By sharing bite-sized road maps with your students throughout a school day or school year, you are helping them to succeed. "Bite-size" can be defined as 3-5 clear steps, with a target of three. As we've already mentioned, clarified expectations foster routine, predictability and ultimately, a sense of safety. Be sure that instructional objectives are posted and communicated. Is your class schedule visible and correct? Do you refer to it throughout the day? Are station areas and supplies labeled (using rebus indicators, where necessary)? How often do you review key routines? Check your day for clarity. Define and refine.

4. **Trust:**

   Trust that students are wholly capable of making great choices and doing the right thing. Does that mean perfection? No. It does mean that in a healthy, facilitative environment most students, most of the time, will strive to meet the expectations set by (and modeled by) the teacher. We are intentional about setting the bar high, because that's where students will reach. Maintain confidence that they will stretch to achieve it. As students see that you trust them, they will begin living up to the expectation that they are probably doing the right thing. They will almost always respond by trusting you in return. Aim for autonomy. Give away power (when appropriate). Expect greatness.

5. **Practice Problem Solving:**

   Investigation that relies upon solution seeking engages students in developing deeper concept understanding and creative thinking abilities, while also building essential life skills. Problem-solving behaviors are learned. They are either explicitly taught or modeled by others. The school is an ideal incubator for nurturing these attributes. Offer specific steps toward solving a problem. Model these thoughts and behavior patterns. Provide multiple opportunities for students to practice problem solving in a variety of subjects and contexts. View problems as "puzzles". Solution seeking is a willed behavior. Our role is to guide the discovery of enjoyment and creative thinking in these processes.

6. **Teach Critical Social Skills:**

   Young people often need to be taught how to interact in positive ways. This is especially true in a Newcomer context, where layers of cultural expectation overlap one another. Essential social skills encompass sensitivity, empathy, humor, reliability, honesty, respect, and concern. Learners often benefit from explicit step-by-step social routines that work through these skill sets. Modeling, play-acting, and "Looks Like/Sounds Like/Feels Like" charts are also useful. Plan lessons to incorporate openings to explore and practice social skills. Offer guidance, and get out of the way. Provide cuing only when relevant. Share constructive feedback and reinforcement of positive behaviors. *Be* the way you wish your students to behave.

7. **Embrace "Failure" as a Success:**

   Trying requires immense courage. Perceived failure is a byproduct of trying. If we look at a FAIL- a First Attempt In Learning, then we are able to see that we have many more possible tries ahead of us. When we work to remove the fear of failing, we are also working to embed a confidence in trying. In my own classroom, we celebrate our failures outright. "Did you succeed the way you hoped you were going to?" *No*. "Did you learn something?" *Yes*. "Bravo! You are a successful learner." Next time you fail at something, try acknowledging it in front of your students. Observe aloud what might have occurred and what part of your strategy you might change to bring about a different result. Failure is simply feedback. If we can take some wisdom from it, and adjust our sails, failure is a sure step in the right direction of success. Aim to create safety nets for trying.

8. **Acknowledge Progress:**

A simple acknowledgement of our gains can go a long way. When we feel appreciated in our efforts, we also feel empowered to continue on a positive trajectory. Administrators, teachers, bus drivers, custodians, cafeteria personnel and afterschool care teams perform better in supportive environments where they feel that they are a contributive factor to the overarching success of a network. Our students, not surprisingly, also thrive in these settings.

Progress has an infinite number of faces. Growth and change can occur in every facet of learning- in academic, linguistic, social, emotional and cultural capacities. Take the time to offer a thank you for a student's concentrated efforts. Post students' work, along with encouraging and reflective feedback. Share students' growth. Acknowledge healthy choice making, positive social behaviors and persistence in the light of adversity. Help all learners to discover, refine and purposely engage their strongest attributes, and seek equity in endorsing successes publicly. Each day, relish in small miracles.

Looking for more ideas on how to incorporate students' heritage cultures in the classroom? *The Newcomer Student* is full of them. Chapters 5-8 provide a number of resources with regard to cultural nuances, classroom exercises and multicultural reading lists. Additional tools, news and plans can be found on our website, at refugeeclassroom.com.

9 SIGNIFICANT STRESS & TRAUMA: IDENTIFICATION & MITIGATION

> **Guiding Questions for Chapter 9:**
> -- What is our team's vision for addressing the mental health of our students?
> -- How are students with significant stress identified in our district and/or building?
> -- Who are our mental health resource personnel? Who do we refer our students to? What does the referral process look like?
> -- What tools do teachers currently have to address and/or mitigate significant stress in the classroom? How are teachers supported in these aims?
> -- What room do we have to grow and improve in this capacity? How will our efforts benefit our students?
> -- What steps can we take now to achieve these aims?

Numerous studies have shown that refugee children are at high risk of a broad range of psychological problems including depression, behavioural problems, aggression, anxiety, and post-traumatic stress disorder (PTSD).
– Author Marc Herman

"All children experience stress," reflects Dr. Andra Brill, ELA Network partner at Denver Public Schools. "Children experience stressful events each day and throughout the day. Very few stressful events are actually traumatic. We have to be careful with how we utilize the language of trauma."

From, *The Newcomer Student: An Educator's Guide to Aid Transition*, we recall:
"Stressful life events…can affect mental health and induce behavior-related changes in children. Physical transition can result in diminished control and loss of familiar guideposts, especially when the change is unanticipated. If and when abrupt transition threatens to overwhelm an individual's accessible coping resources, then mental functioning can be compromised."

The text continues,

> "Stressors related to the refugee experience prompt aggravated internal responses, which may exceed reactive norms, and consequently overwhelm an individual's emotional, social, and cognitive capacities. As self-ownership and sense-making capabilities are diminished, post-traumatic stress can occur."

Stress is natural and very often healthy. Significant trauma, meanwhile, devastates the capacity to negotiate stress and restore normative status. *Transition shock* is a broader umbrella that encompasses both of these values, normative stress and acute stress. For the purpose of clarity, this text will rely on the term *transition shock* to referencing stress and trauma-related indicators.

Transition Shock

Many refugee and immigrant Newcomers will experience some type or degree of transition shock. Transition shock is a broad value that encompasses culture shock, traumatic distress, Post Traumatic Stress Syndrome (PTSS) and similar socially disabling patterns. These types of traumatic upset are processed in predictable ways, even while correlating outward manifestations are exceedingly individualized.

Jan Kizilhan, of the University of Duhok, Germany explains:

"Children can fall victim to a kind of conditional shock - they get scared and become unsettled. The other aspect is that their parents, confronted with war, with torture, with soldiers and attacks, are helpless. Up to that point, their children had learned that their parents could defend and protect them. Suddenly, this social configuration is flipped on its head. Their bond to their parents and environment is thereby destroyed. Fleeing war is, from a psychological perspective, a deep gash, and in the worst case, it can lead to these children never being able to rid themselves of that experience."

Transition shock, including trauma, moves through projected stages of processing. The most significant, and generally longest enduring, of these stages is grief. Grief is usually brought on by extreme, unanticipated loss and bears an independent cycle within the larger trauma management context. There is overwhelming evidence that unusually pronounced or prolonged grief has the capacity to add an entire additional phase to the human life cycle. Individuals can become "stuck" in this phase for variable periods of time.

The stages of traumatic grief are three-pronged and involve: *avoidance* (denial and resistance), *assimilation* (includes silent-period, obstructed speech, re-presentation, survivor's guilt and reactive fear), and *accommodation* (acknowledgement and growth capacity). In the classroom setting, transition shock manifests in a variety of ways that include speech impediments, nightmares, incontinence, extreme sleepiness, inability to concentrate, social withdrawal and other loss-oriented behaviors.

In *The Newcomer Student*, we describe these stress indicators such that,

"Our students demonstrate an array of stress indicators, many of which are nonverbal. These include irritability, sleepiness, restlessness, aggression, withdrawn personality, bedwetting, concentration difficulties, diminished school performance, hoarding, and high-risk behavior. Stress-induced tendencies can manifest in any individual, and are not limited by age, gender, race, or circumstance.

Manifestations of Transition Shock

Headaches	Speech Impediments	Social Withdrawal
Nausea	Incontinence	Boredom
Compulsive Tidiness	Extreme Disorganization	Uncontrolled Weepiness
Excessive Sleepiness	Uncontrolled Bowel Urges	Appetite Changes
Concentration Difficulties	Sensitivity to Stimuli	Inability to Keep Friends
Defiance	Delinquency	Resistance
Clinginess	Debilitating Homesickness	Toe-walking
"W" sitting	Bed Wetting	Self-harm
Socially Inappropriate Behaviors	Inability to Control Emotions	Balance & Coordination Challenges
Difficulty Planning	Attendance Concerns	Challenges with Automatized Behaviors

© The Newcomer Fieldbook, 2017

Transition Shock Scorecard

- ☐ Headaches
- ☐ Speech Impediments
- ☐ Social Withdrawal
- ☐ Nausea
- ☐ Incontinence
- ☐ Boredom
- ☐ Compulsive Tidiness
- ☐ Excessive disorganization
- ☐ Uncontrolled weepiness
- ☐ Excessive sleepiness
- ☐ Uncontrolled bowel urges
- ☐ Appetite changes
- ☐ Concentration difficulties
- ☐ Sensitivity to stimuli
- ☐ Inability to keep friends
- ☐ Defiance
- ☐ Delinquency
- ☐ Resistance
- ☐ Clinginess
- ☐ Debilitating homesickness
- ☐ Toe-walking
- ☐ "W" sitting
- ☐ Bed wetting
- ☐ Self-harm
- ☐ Socially inappropriate behaviors
- ☐ Inability to control emotions
- ☐ Balance/Co-ordination challenges
- ☐ Difficulty planning
- ☐ Attendance concerns
- ☐ Challenges with automated behaviors (i.e., hand-raising, changing tasks)

Transition Shock Manifestations: Student Evaluation

Total Number of Indicators Marked _____

0-5: Mild Manifestations- Observable behaviors may be attributed to any number of common or uncommon stressors or may be attributed to an individual's personality. Immediate interventions are not recommended. Continued evaluation is recommended.

5-10: Mild-Mid Manifestations- Observable behaviors may be attributed to any number of stressors or personality traits, and may include minimal trauma-influenced anxiety. Immediate interventions are not recommended. Continued evaluation is recommended.

10-15: Mid-level Manifestations- Observable behaviors may be attributed to common stressors and/or personality traits, and are likely to include some trauma-influenced anxiety. Consideration for interventions is recommended. Continued evaluation is necessary.

15-20: Mid-High Manifestations- Observable behaviors are very likely to be influenced by stress, and may be indicative of moderate traumatic impact. Timely, consistent, research-based interventions are recommended. Partnerships with school-centered counsel are advised. Continued evaluation is critical.

25-31: High Level Manifestations- Observable behaviors are very likely to be influenced by stress, and may be indicative of significant traumatic impact. Timely, consistent, research-based interventions are recommended. Partnerships with school-centered counsel and/or medical practitioners are advised. Continued evaluation is critical.

TRIGGERED ANXIETY: THE RCA4T SURVEY

Many countries across the globe are making great strides in healthy refugee resettlement, integration and education. Canada, for example, continues to set a high standard in its intake and resettlement initiatives. Meanwhile, a tremendous amount of Newcomer-based research and strategic innovation is currently taking place in Europe and Turkey.

REFUGEE Class Assistance 4 Teachers (RCA4T) is a leader in this arena. The co-operative task force involves partners from 5 different countries, namely Turkey, Bulgaria, Greece, Serbia and Belgium. The goal of the initiative is to "create training material which will enable teachers to cope with the challenges that are derived from the integration of migrant and refugee children in education."

As a research component of one of its key projects, the organization issued an education-based survey. RCA4T employs the data to investigate and produce solutions around the "challenges teachers face when they have children in their class with a refugee background." The RCA4T survey, in itself, is a valuable tool.

A key segment of the questionnaire invites teachers to observe and record student-evidenced anxiety and/or behavior reactions to specific environmental triggers. With RCA4T's permission, the survey points have been reformatted into a classroom-ready information-gathering resource. The wording of the checklist comes directly from the RCA4T questionnaire. Meanwhile, the scorecard has been produced separately, as part of this text.

In the same vein as the Transition Shock Scorecard, this checklist is purposed as an instrument for collecting additional information about students' background and learning preferences. It has been formulated with the specific needs and possible experiences of refugee Newcomers in mind. Of course, population overlap may occur. That is, students of any background or nationality may evidence anxiety triggers as identified in this document; significant stress does demonstrate exclusivity.

Triggered Anxiety at School Scorecard

- ☐ Dark corridors
- ☐ People wearing uniforms or heavy boots
- ☐ Loud or harsh talking
- ☐ Bells, fire alarms or evacuation drills
- ☐ Not understanding the host language, or other languages children speak outside the classroom
- ☐ Items associated with seasonal holidays, such as masks and skeletons at Halloween, or Christmas/New Year outfits, firecrackers or fireworks
- ☐ Other children staring at them
- ☐ Evacuation procedures or "lockdowns"
- ☐ Racism
- ☐ Body language that may be misinterpreted
- ☐ Situations that may seem out of control, like children "horsing around"
- ☐ Too many instructions
- ☐ Sound of strong footsteps
- ☐ Sitting too long
- ☐ Groups of children talking loudly
- ☐ On-going confusing noise, chaos
- ☐ Abrupt changes
- ☐ Raised fist threats, confrontations
- ☐ Communicate from a distance without engagement
- ☐ Screaming
- ☐ New adult in the classroom with no explanation of why and who
- ☐ Increased or continued frustration of adult
- ☐ Sirens
- ☐ Physical restraint
- ☐ Yelling, bullying
- ☐ Forced separation from parent
- ☐ Signing forms
- ☐ Disclosing personal or family details
- ☐ Revealing personal details or information
- ☐ Requested/required signatures

RCA4T Survey- Triggered Anxiety at School: Student Evaluation

Total Number of Indicators Marked _____

0-5: Mild Manifestations- Observable behaviors may be attributed to any number of common or uncommon stressors or may be attributed to an individual's personality. Immediate interventions are not recommended. Continued evaluation is recommended.

5-10: Mild-Mid Manifestations- Observable behaviors may be attributed to any number of stressors or personality traits, and may include *minimal anxiety*. Immediate interventions are not recommended. Continued evaluation is recommended.

10-15: Mid-level Manifestations- Observable behaviors may be attributed to common stressors and/or personality traits, and are likely to include *some anxiety*. Consideration for interventions is recommended. Continued evaluation is necessary.

15-20: Mid-High Manifestations- Observable behaviors are very likely to be influenced by stress, and which may be indicative of *moderate anxiety*. Timely, consistent, research-based interventions are recommended. Partnerships with school-centered counsel are advised. Continued evaluation is critical.

25-31: High Level Manifestations- Observable behaviors are very likely to be influenced by stress, and which may be indicative of *significant anxiety*. Timely, consistent, research-based interventions are recommended. Partnerships with school-centered counsel and/or medical practitioners are advised. Continued evaluation is critical.

Traumatic Stress & Brain Development

Trauma occurs when an individual is exposed to an event or series of events that are so significant that they overwhelm a person's resources to effectively manage the stress. In *The Newcomer Student*, we talked about it in this way: "Stressors related to the refugee experience prompt aggravated internal responses, which may exceed relative norms, and consequently overwhelm an individual's emotional, social, and cognitive capacities. As self-ownership and sense-making capabilities are diminished, post-traumatic stress can occur."

Significant stress affects the human brain in explicit ways that can manifest as physiological, psychological and emotional deterrents to social, academic and economic well-being. The brain itself compartmentalizes stress and trauma, and does so in two primary zones: the combined brain stem and limbic area and the cerebral cortex. Damage to either or both of these regions can significantly impair learning and integration success, and therefore, must be appropriately addressed as part of the framework for effective refugee and immigrant Newcomer educational programming.

Together, the brain stem and limbic system comprise the emotional center of the brain and are responsible for integrating sensory input, emotional regulation, storing and retrieval of memories, regulating focus and producing responses to stimuli. When this region of the brain is compromised, the low-level functions it controls are disrupted. Refugee Newcomer learners are at an exceptional risk for limbic dysfunction. This is critical in the context of learning and frequently manifests as emotional outbursts, incontinence, toe-walking, lack of balance and coordination, W-sitting (sitting on knees with shins splayed to the side), fine and gross motor lapses, and lack of organizational skills.

The cerebral cortex, which wraps around the limbic system, occupies the greatest area in the brain and is sub-divided into the right and left hemispheres. Many hypotheses exist around precise personality traits linked to right and left-brain functioning; a similar number of rebukes counter them. Scientific evidence does provide us with a few certainties that also serve as grounding factors in the design and implementation of effective Newcomer language-learning curricula.

The right brain develops in advance of the left-brain and is typically associated with traits related to emotionality and creativity. Along with the amygdala, the right brain oversees lower-hierarchy behaviors that become automatic with training, such as: adhering to social norms, sitting on cue, or raising a hand to ask a question. The right brain reads observable cues, such as body language, gestures and facial expressions. It identifies with negative responses and stimulates withdrawal.

Right brain functions can be best observed in small children. In observing children between the ages of one and five, curiosity, creativity and elementary automaticity are usually evident. The left-brain has not yet fully developed.

The left-brain, then, is concerned with higher-level functions. It is associated with logic and organizational factors and has been demonstrated to process and respond to positive stimuli. With regard to Newcomer learners, left- brain functions are critical to language development. Words and word meanings are filtered and digested through the left-brain.

Right and left brain capacities are relevant in the context of refugee Newcomer education for the reason that student learning and integration success is dependent upon the functionality of both hemispheres; and traumatic stress, as frequently observed in such populations, disrupts traditional growth patterns in the brain hemispheres. Namely, developments within the right brain can be suspended, stopped, or even reversed. Affected individuals can become "stuck" in lower-hierarchy behavior patterns.

When maturation of the right brain is impeded, even preliminary developments of the left-brain are abnegated. As a result, language-learning functions are compromised or entirely denied. This means that even our best instructional efforts are futile in the absence of trauma-mitigating practices.

TRANSITION SHOCK & COGNITIVE FUNCTION

Significant shock can impair cognitive function. Kaplan and his team are among the leading researchers in this arena. *Cognitive assessment of refugee children: Effects of trauma and new language acquisition* (Transcultural Psychiatry, 2015) examines possible outcomes of traumatic stress on cerebral capacity. Individuals can be deeply impacted in the areas of:

- ☐ Understanding instructions
- ☐ Problem-solving
- ☐ Self-regulation
- ☐ Creativity
- ☐ Memory
- ☐ Motivation
- ☐ Anticipation of success
- ☐ Anticipation of failure
- ☐ Reflection
- ☐ Categorizing
- ☐ Ability to accept adult guidance

Here's what else we know- transition shock negatively impacts school performance. In fact, significant stress is linked to:

- ☐ Increased rate of school absences
- ☐ Increased school drop-out rate
- ☐ Increase in student suspensions
- ☐ Increase in student expulsions
- ☐ Decrease in student GPA
- ☐ Decrease in student reading level

In other words, we are not in a position to neglect the influences of significant stress among students. We cannot compromise our responsibility to mitigate transition shock in the school setting. To do so would be to compromise our very students and our core values as educators. The good news is that we *can* have a positive impact. Transition shock, in most cases, can be overcome. We have the opportunity to collaborate in this process.

MITIGATING TRAUMA & SHOCK IN ACADEMIC SETTINGS

Traumatic stress and shock are serious conditions that may require direct psychological counseling and care. However, significant stress can be both proactively and reactively addressed in the classroom setting as an important support to professional mental health evaluation. Correspondingly, refugee Newcomer educational frameworks can benefit from integrating trauma mitigation techniques.

A healthy, positive school climate is paramount to stress-dissolution efforts. Classroom teachers can be trained to recognize symptoms of traumatic stress and shock, and to buffer these manifestations and to refer specific students for advanced psychological services. For example, by limiting exposure to external sensory stimuli, teachers can reduce trauma-related episodes in the classroom. Routine and predictability are also fundamental to stress dissolution.

There also exists a correlation between an increase in teacher-student one-on-one time and a decrease in students' stress manifestations. We can refer to this practice as, "time in vs. time out". Stress is mitigated by social incorporation and enhanced by isolation, especially when negative behaviors are evidenced. In short, trauma affected individuals typically respond in positive ways to positive relationships.

Some of the most promising school-based antipodes to trauma involve crossing midline (or bilateral integration) activities. These practices, which can be explicitly taught and modeled in classroom settings, encourage right and left-brain communication, sensory integration, and emotional regulation. Crossing midline activities engage participants in traversing imaginary lines that divide the human body into quadrants, such as touching right elbow to left knee. Surprisingly, many children demonstrate difficulty in completing midline-crossing tasks and require practice to improve.

Other bilateral integration ideas include:

- ☐ Criss-cross-crawls: Crawling while touching opposite elbow to knee
- ☐ Drawing infinity signs (sideways figure eights) through the air with hands, arms, toes, heads
- ☐ Playing with cars, trains, planes in looped, zigzag and circular paths
- ☐ Washing (or pretend washing) large objects
- ☐ Criss-cross hand clapping games
- ☐ Dancing, ribbon twirling, scarf twirling
- ☐ Stacking games
- ☐ Opposites: tapping right hand to left shoulder/reverse; touching right elbow to left knee or ankle/reverse; touching right fingers to left toes/reverse
- ☐ Body swings: swing right leg over to left side/reverse; swing upper body to the left side/reverse.
- ☐ Partner coordination exercises like "Boom/Snap/Clap" for older students: https://www.youtube.com/watch?v=lBSteR_0vdQ
- ☐ Tracing
- ☐ Grapevines
- ☐ Twister
- ☐ Sorting activities, using only one hand at a time

Mitigating Trauma & Grief in the Classroom

Routine and predictability create calm and safety. When students feel secure, energy can be directed away from overwhelming concern and toward active school engagement. The following elements promote feelings of safety and routine in the classroom environment.

- Calm, organized environment
    - Established classroom areas
    - Labeled supplies
    - Calm teacher behaviors
    - Designated "safe" spaces in the school and classroom
- Reduced sensory stimuli
    - Moderated volumes
    - Appropriate lighting
    - Purposeful classroom decoration/design
- Routine and predictability
    - Posted daily schedule
    - Advance warning for schedule shifts, where possible
    - Advance explanation and practice for non-routine events, such as fire drills and lock-downs
- Opportunities for guided choice
- Deferred re-enactments
    - Children who have encountered trauma may instigate friction with adults as a vehicle to recreate unhealthy traumatic experiences. It is important to recognize and redirect such behaviors.
- "Time In" vs. "Time Out"
    - Focusing on addressing unhealthy behaviors through conversation and positive attention, rather than social isolation
- PBIS (Positive Behavior Interventions & Supports) systems
    - Resources: www.pbis.org; www.educationworld.com/a_admin/admin/admin535.shtml
- Efforts to promote cross-cultural understanding
- Art, writing, song and drama as therapeutic learning tools
- Crossing midline activities
    - Research indicates that significant trauma can cause right brain stalls or regressions in development. Crossing midline activities may help strengthen right brain activity and create bridges to the left-brain, where language acquisition occurs.
    - "Brain breaks" throughout the school day
    - Resources: 1.therapystreetforkids.com/CrossingMidline 2.ot-mom-learning-activities.com/activities-for-crossing-the-midline 3.growinghandsonkids.com/crossing-midline-exercises-for-kids
- Timely referrals for advanced care
- Self-care: The most important aspect of all!

DBT HOUSES

The following exercise comes from the book, *Dialectical Behavior Therapy Skills: 101 Mindfulness Exercises and Other Fun Activities for Children and Adolescents* (R & K Christensen, 2009). This art-therapy centered task is extremely helpful in working through stress and opening lines of trustful conversation. I have personally employed this technique with very young children, teens and adults, with very successful results each time.

Here's what I love about DBT (Dialectical Behavioral Therapy) skills. First, they can be implemented in a whole class setting without specifically singling out stress-impacted individuals. Second, they can be very revealing for all students and can provide terrific insights into our students' lives and thinking patterns. Third, they can be used in a variety of ways to facilitate healthy discussion, connection, empathy and creative solution seeking.

This exercise invites participants to construct a house. A number of printable templates exist online for this purpose. However, I prefer to have participants draw their own, as this process is both an extension of art therapy and revealing in terms of house design. After introducing the activity from either a trust-building, goal-setting or solution-seeking perspective, I provide plain white copy paper and an array of markers.

The activity is guided in this way:

"Today I am going to ask you to draw a house. This house represents you and your thoughts. You do not have to share your house with me or with your neighbors. I'm also going to give you instructions as you build your house. Please listen as you draw and write.

Now you will begin. Please use most of your paper to draw your house. Your house needs four items: a roof, a door, a chimney and a billboard. As you draw, please create a roof. Please make a door. Be sure that your house has a chimney. It must also have a billboard. A billboard is a sign. You can place the sign on the roof, in the yard, hanging from a window, or in another place that calls to you."

I wait for participants to complete this section, usually showing a template house as they work. This house is available for free download at http://childhoodinterventions.blogspot.com/2014/12/dbt-house.html is a good example.

I then guide students through the DBT House prompts. This version included is directly exported from Kim's Counseling Corner and can be easily located at http://www.kimscounselingcorner.com/therapeutic-activities/self-exploration-using-a-dbt-house.

While students are working, I remind them they may find a directive or part of the house that resonates or feels uncomfortable and to be aware of those areas as they come up. When we reach the door, I usually offer the option of "writing those ideas in the mind" if it is too uncomfortable to put them to paper.

Parts of the House:

Foundation: On the floor of the house, write the values that govern your life. *(Note: As I walk students through this activity, I usually paraphrase based on participant age and language level. For example, in differentiating for ELLs- I might say, "Write words that tell about what you think it means to be a good person").*

Walls: Along the walls, write anything or anyone who supports you. *(Write names or words for people who are helpful in your life.)*

Roof: On the roof, name the things or people that protect you.

Door: Write the things that you keep hidden from others. *(What are the things about yourself that you don't want to tell other people?)*

Chimney: Coming out of the chimney, write down ways in which you blow off steam. *(What do you do when you are sad, mad, frustrated or have too much energy?)*

Billboard: On the billboard, write the things you are proud of and want others to see.

Credit: Kim's Counseling Corner, 2016

In working with younger students, I stop here. Even this small bit of student investment can be incredible insightful. Are there parents, teachers or other adults in the roof? Are the walls bare or full of life? What is coming out of the chimney? *I hit my little brother…I cut myself…I play soccer?* What do students want to reveal?

In an elementary context, we are likely to share our results in an "inside-outside circle" format. *Share something on your billboard that you are proud of. Name a person or thing that you wrote on your walls.* Students often find so much common ground here. Again, I reserve the "door" for one-on-one conversation, when useful and relevant.

As for middle school and high school students, they may be more hesitant to reveal anything beyond the surface level. In working with older participants, I make a point to ensure that these are private and personal constructions, not to be shared unless a person volunteers it. We put up "offices" made of folders as we build our houses.

Then, we explore our constructs using a "Numbered/Labeled Corners" technique (a Gradient Line works well here, too). *Walk to and stand under the picture in the room that matches the place in your house you feel most confident about. Stand in the area you felt the most discomfort in walking through. Walk to the location where you had the most ideas or things to write about.* Again, students are often surprised to find themselves in plenty of company. From here, we can begin to make a path for healthy conversation and connection.

In working with older students, I invite then to continue on with the DBT House exercise by dividing their house into 4 layers. They are prompted as follows:

Levels of the House:

Level 1: List behaviors that you are trying to gain control over or areas of your life you want to change.

Level 2: List or draw emotions you want to experience more often, more fully, or in a more healthy way.

Level 3: List all the things you are happy about or want to feel happy about.

Level 4: List or draw what a "Life Worth Living" would look like for you. *(In other words, what is the goal or ideal outcome?)*

Credit: Kim's Counseling Corner, 2016

To close this chapter, we'll examine four sample DBT houses. I'd love to hear how the DBT House approach has served you in working with students. Please share at @RefugeeClassroom!

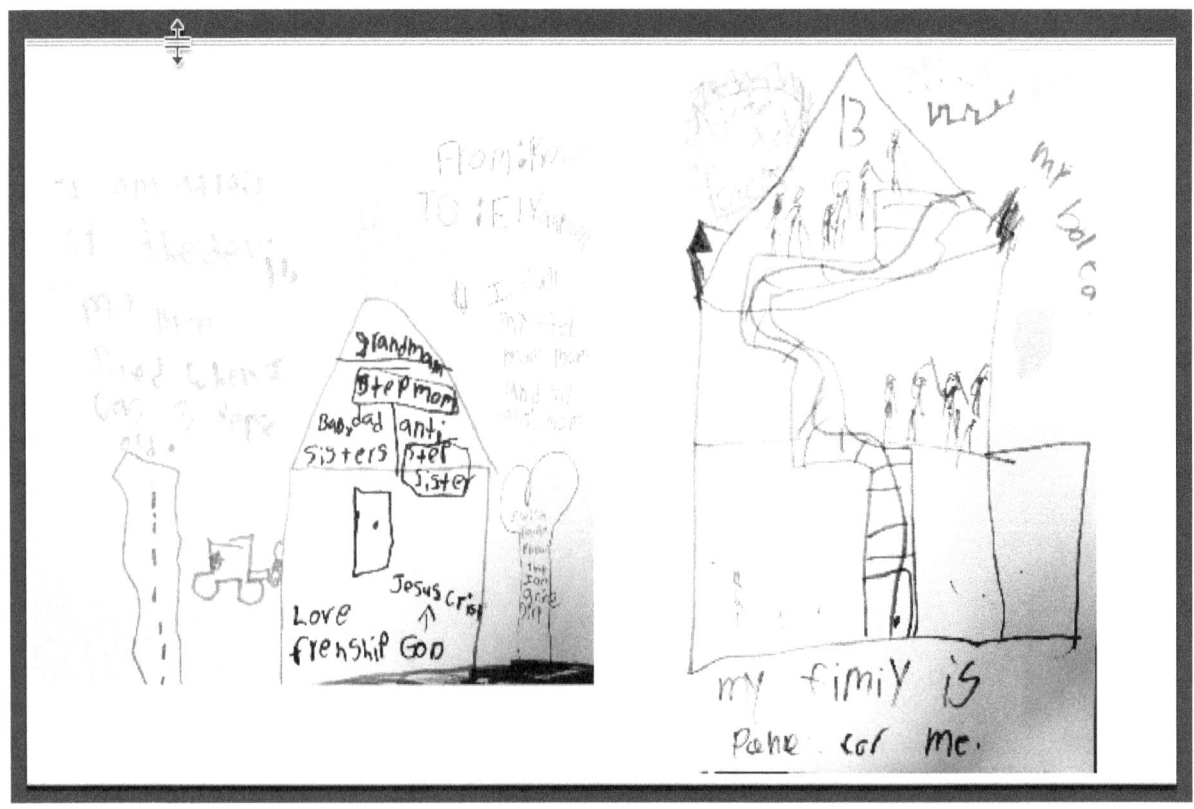

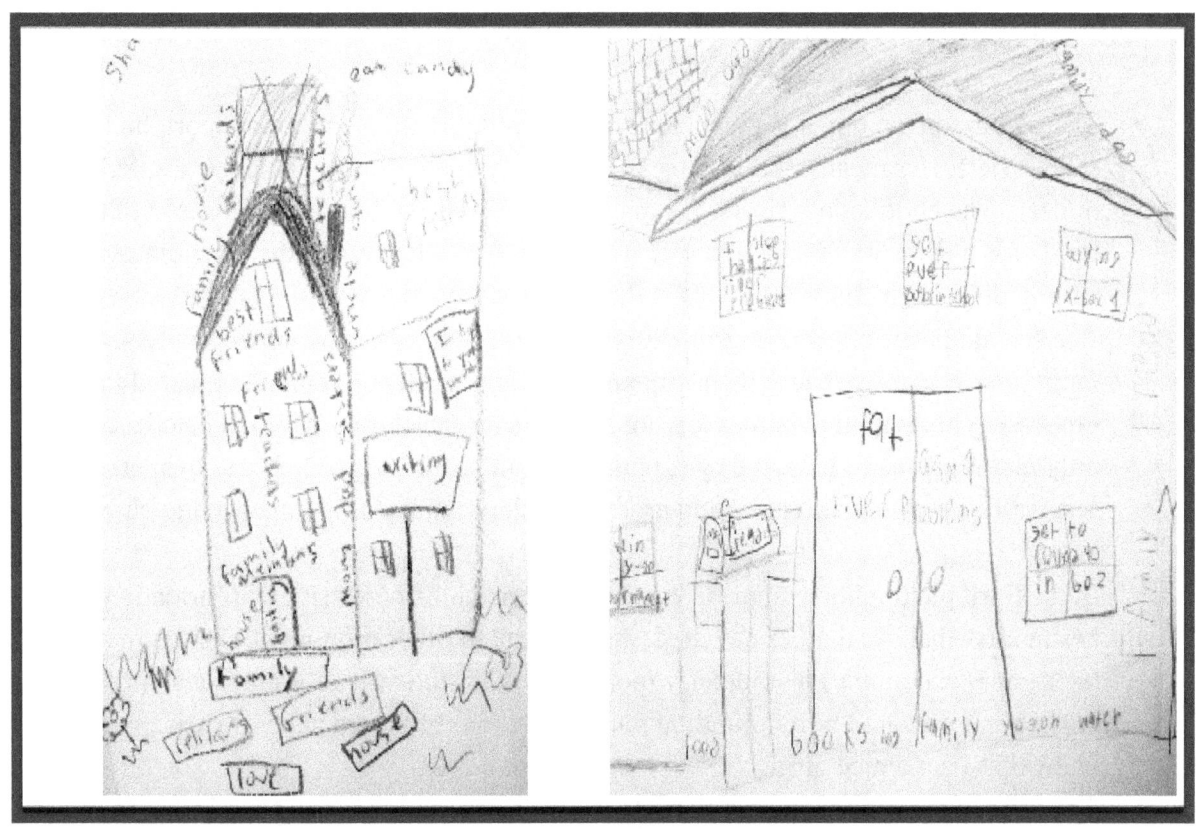
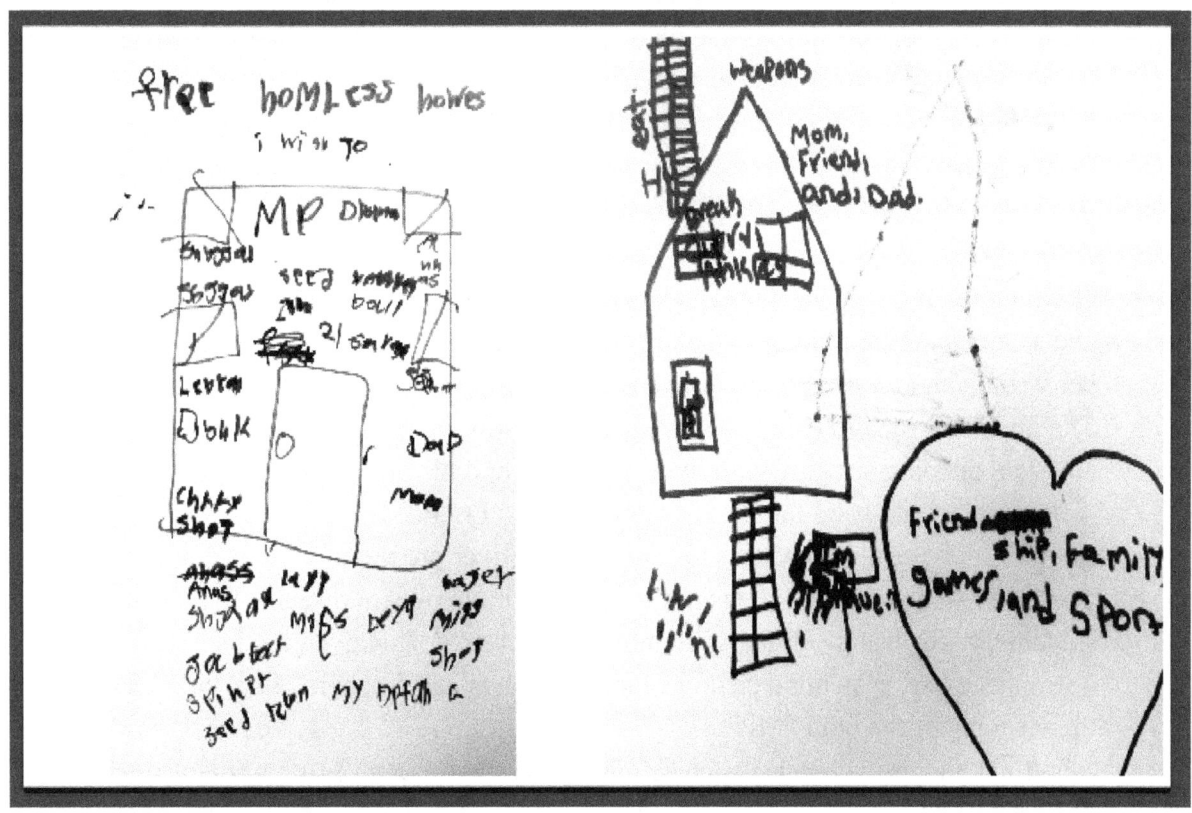

Thoughts and Wonderings, Elementary Grades:

- The picture on the upper right appears quite healthy, with plenty of support, including school staff. Her means of releasing stress is to "punch pillows and cry" (a safe, healthy outlet). The child's door reads, "I am embarrassed of my brother". However, the brother is also featured as a support. This issue was later resolved with mom as typical sibling disagreements.
- The second house appears angry, with furrowed eyebrows. The upper text reads, "My family protects me because the roof explode." This student (Yemen) appeared to be processing his truth that homes are not always safe structures. Mom is listed as the only major source of help and/or support. "Mom" is also recorded, and then erased on one wall. The foundation (written around the door reads, "It is important to share and be nice."
- In the third picture, the author (Congo) felt the need to share critical information about her family- that her mother had died, that she called other prominent women in her life (step-mom and auntie) by motherly monikers. The student's religion is also prominent feature and seems to be a grounding value. The tree/billboard states, "I wish people knew that I am a nice girl."
- The last house (Mexico) was a first glimpse at this child's bustling home life, where immediate and extended family members and friends live in and visit. "Family" is also the only truly legible word in the picture, outside of the students name, indicating that family is at once a foundational value, support and source of protection.

Thoughts and Wonderings, Upper Grades:

- The picture on the upper right appears healthy, with plenty of supports. Family, friends and school staff are represented and she has many foundational values. She is proud of her writing and relieves stress and tension by eating candy. Her hope is to graduate.
- The upper left picture (Mexico) revealed interesting news to me regarding the student's apparent ongoing struggle with liver problems, and his internal perception of his weight. Mom, dad and family are represented. "Friend" is recorded, indicating a singular individual. He wishes to "stop having liver problems". He is a proud reader.
- The lower left picture (Syria) is quite scattered in thought and seems to indicate that the student lives or has lived in a "free homeless house". However, he does seem to have a strong support system made up of family, friends and teachers. I am curious about the meaning of the bold "MP".
- The final picture (Iraq) also appears mostly healthy, though I find it interesting that "weapons" is featured prominently in the protection area of the house (Iraq). The symbol in the door drives my curiosity. The student enjoys his personal relationships, games and sports and relieves stress by eating.

10 IMPACTFUL INSTRUCTIONAL MOVES

> Guiding questions for Chapter 10:
> -- How do we, as a team, define "optimal" instruction for language learners? For all learners?
> -- What techniques do we already implement with fidelity and/or efficacy on our campus? What are the results of those practices?
> -- Who on our campus is knowledgeable and/or successful in this area? How can we leverage the expertise of these individuals?
> -- How do or can we support growth for all school staff in this regard? What strides do we make to promote language learning as a school-wide focus?
> -- How do we measure the success (or need for improvement) related to implementation of sheltered instruction techniques? In what ways are administrators, teachers, and students held accountable for language learning?
> -- What other questions or suggestions come up? Share those out @RefugeeClassroom and @NewcomerESL!

Specific strategies and tools lend themselves to best practices in education, including Newcomer-ESL instruction. We'll work through these in alphabetical order. Several of the following resources have already been introduced in *The Newcomer Student*. The goal, in this section, is to provide insight as to how ELL theory can be put into effective practice.

Experiment with the following exercises. Those that work for you, combine with the other successful instructional strategies you already have in place. Then, invest in adjusting, refining, and building as necessary. Often, our most effective instructional practices are not wholly self-derived. Instead, they "show up" through mentors, peer practitioners, students, reading (of other people's ideas), and a lot of trial-and-error (bolstered by student, peer and administrator feedback). Our craft is a work in progress. Here are a few more tools for the toolbox.

"Big 10" Newcomer Classroom Reminders

1. Classroom culture drives learning. Newcomer students thrive in classrooms that are safe, structured and predictable.
2. Content Language Objectives guide lesson planning and ground student understanding throughout the lesson.
3. With regard to lesson planning, aim for relevance and quality, not quantity.
4. Speech should be clear, deliberate and unrushed. Louder or painfully slowed speech is not helpful.
5. Gestures can be used to enforce an idea, but should be minimized with time. Where possible, normalized gestures should be used.
6. Language learners often require a longer "wait-time" in producing a response. After asking a question, allow for up to two minutes of unprompted thinking time. If a student is not yet ready, offer opportunities for production, such as think-pair-share.
7. Labeling, visuals, realia, manipulatives, graphic organizers, sentence frames and hands-on exploration are essential to the successful Newcomer classroom experience. Each of these is a language-building path toward content accessibility.
8. Cooperative structures encourage language development, enhance positive classroom culture and put students in the drivers' seats of their own learning. Learn to get out of the way!
9. Newcomer students may be working through trauma, shock or other stressors. Monitoring external stimuli can help mitigate significant stress. Learn to recognize symptoms and know when to ask for help.
10. You may be your student's first teacher, or the first teacher in America. So, smile! Show welcoming. Be what you wish for your students to become.

© The Newcomer Fieldbook, 2017

I: Academic Language & ELD

Language learning engages some of our most complex cognitive capacities. From Flora Lewis: "Learning another language is not only learning different words for the same things, but learning another way to think about things." Thus, language instruction requires that we teach words as well as the processes of thinking about language and vocabulary.

Growing our understanding of how language acquisition works helps us to better address the needs of our new-to-English learners. Michael Willis, writing for Southeast Education Network, notes: "Academic Language is believed to be one of the most important factors in the academic success of English Language Learners, and it has been shown to be a major contributor to achievement gaps between ELLs and English-proficient students."

We'll examine language acquisition under two distinct umbrellas: English Language Development (ELD) and Academic Language. The first refers to conversational language use and function (social expressiveness); the latter addresses content-specific communication. New-to-English speakers typically achieve conversational language fluency at or around two years of practice, while academic language proficiency can take five to seven years to develop.

ELD | Academic

Language Learning

ELD	Academic
Explicit teaching of language use and function; critical for social communication and interpersonal success	Explicit teaching of content and discipline-specific vocabulary; critical for comprehension and academic success

ENGLISH LANGUAGE DEVELOPMENT

Teaching for ELLs requires a dedication to English Language Development. ELD instruction is deliberately designed to promote language proficiency and overall school success. As a learner develops an ability to navigate basic language use and function, he or she can begin to access academic language components.

Basic social expressiveness falls under the realm of ELD. These elemental mechanisms of inter-personal communication are essential for successful integration and can be heard in the hallways and lunchrooms and on the bus or playground. Ultimately, the goal of ELD is to provide ELLs a foundation on which academic language constructs can be mapped, built and renovated.

English, in the context of ELD, is explicitly taught using specific strategies that are shown to enhance and accelerate language acquisition. Instruction often occurs in small group settings and focuses on the domains of listening and speaking to build efficacy in the areas of reading and writing. ELD efforts provide opportunities to learn and practice English vocabulary, syntax, conventions, functions, grammar and tone. Student engagement is enhanced through the implementation of sheltered instruction techniques and consistent ongoing feedback toward student growth.

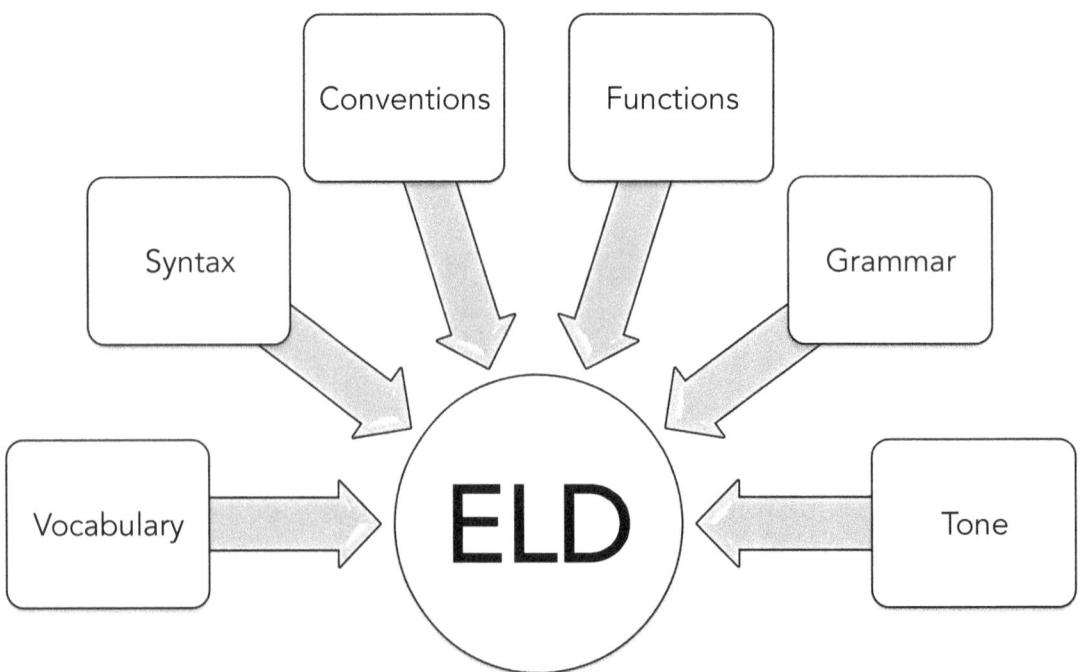

Here's what we can keep in mind about English Language Development:

- It is the basic infrastructure for language learning
- It is necessary for communication
- Language acquisition is the primary goal
- ELD is structured around Tier 1 and Tier 2 words
- ELD instruction should be continued, even as academic language is introduced
- ELD instruction benefits cooperative structures, team building, classroom culture, information processing.
- ELD techniques can be effectively used in whole class settings across a range of language ability levels (including non-ELLs!) to grow command of the English language.

ACADEMIC LANGUAGE

Students require academic language proficiency in order to navigate the classroom experience, to fully participate in content learning, and to express knowledge in school-appropriate ways. Students encounter academic language in learning objectives, textbooks, course/content exercises and standardized testing materials. Writer and researcher Todd Finley summarizes: "Academic language is a meta-language that helps learners acquire the 50,000 words that they are expected to have internalized by the end of high school."

As educators, we can encourage the shift from social language to academic content language in organic ways. One approach is to assist language learners in making conscious moves to "upgrade" known language. In this way, we can scaffold the transition toward advanced content-specific vernacular, or "juicy" words, in elementary teacher talk.

Let's look at some examples in shifting from social to academic language:

- Know: recognize, experience, comprehend
- See: observe, examine, distinguish
- Think: determine, consider, summarize
- Guess: predict, wonder, imagine
- Show: demonstrate, prove, establish
- Write: record, compose, formulate

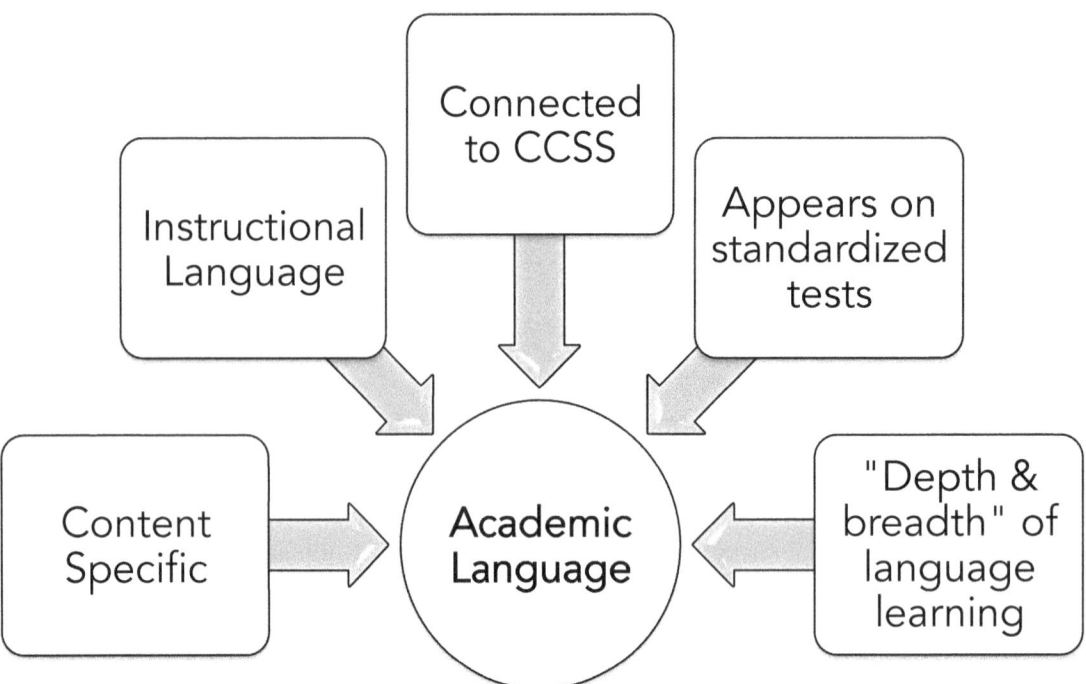

Here's what we can keep in mind about academic language, or *integrated ELD*:

- It is discipline and content specific
- It grows from basic conversational fluency
- Academic language is explicitly taught in direct content context
- It is standards based and essential for school success
- Academic language is structured Tier 2 words and beyond
- Academic language includes and expands upon essential ELD principles (vocabulary, syntax, grammar, conventions and functions)
- Sheltered instruction techniques can also be used for the purpose of teaching and clarifying academic language
- ELD/social language aptitude is not an accurate indicator for academic language proficiency

FITTING IN ALL TOGETHER

It is important to point out that social and academic English need not (and should not) be mutually exclusive entities in the classroom context. Each serves a unique purpose and supports the other. Conversational English is an essential tool for teaching, clarifying and exchanging ideas around academic language.

We can refer to the structure of language building as an "iceberg". At the tip of the iceberg, above the surface, social language proficiency is demonstrated (as output defined by ELD structures). This is what we hear when we engage with our students. It provides a snapshot of an individual's level of BICS (Basic Interpersonal Communication

Skills). Below the surface, we find the deeper, more complex tiers of academic-content language, associated with CALP (Cognitive Academic Language Proficiency). The wide bottom platform of the iceberg represents language mastery.

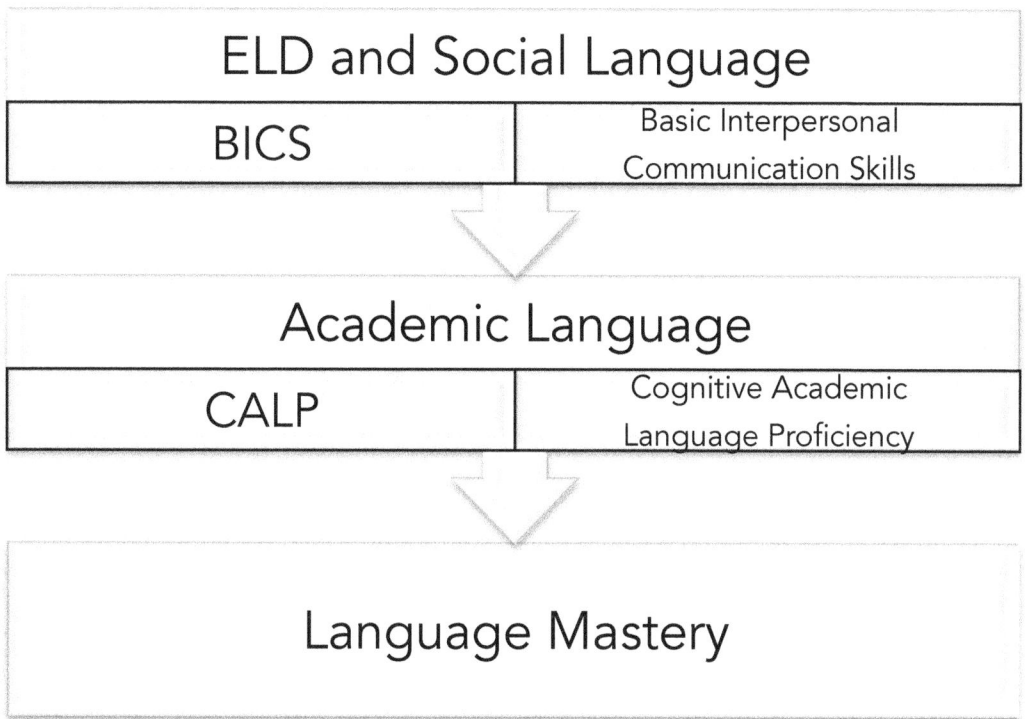

We can make language learning more manageable for our students when we shape our instruction in purposeful and developmentally appropriate ways. That is, we can provide students opportunities to achieve language mastery by building on the brain's tendency to sequentially stack learning according to accessibility and complexity. We show intentionality in our work with language learners by building on known language and scaffolding into new domains.

School success for ELLs requires an integrated approach that combines English Language Development and explicit academic-content language instruction in ways that are tailored to a student's English language capacity at a given time, in a given space. In this way, students are able to work toward the successful negotiation of both worlds on a continuum toward language mastery.

II: Content Language Objectives

Content Language Objectives (CLOs) are a cornerstone of Newcomer instruction. They are also discussed at some length in *The Newcomer Student*. Therefore, we will not dive into great detail here. Instead, I invite you to begin with pages 85-86 in that text.

What we'll say, briefly, is that CLOs drive effective teaching and purposeful learning. They are a non-negotiable. Most school districts agree that CLOs now play a key role in many teacher evaluation systems, from ELA-E to mainstream.

Here, we'll break down and rebuild the Content Language Objective.

Content refers to factual knowledge and understanding of a topic, including conceptualization and critical thinking processes around an academic topic. *Language* encompasses the vocabulary, grammar, syntax, language functions, language structures and academic language structures that students need in order to successfully access content.

From *The Newcomer Student*:

"Simply, *content language objectives define and/or clarify the language necessary to meet the learning goal or content objective.*" When we refer to *language learning objectives*, we are asking the following essential questions:

- What is the function of language in the given (content area) context?
- What language structures are required to achieve the language function?
- What are the prominent concepts of the lesson?
- What key vocabulary words are associated with the context learning?
- What is the current level of students' speech and understanding?"

CLOs can be immensely beneficial in any instructional setting. They are critical in a language-learning context. CLOs "must be made explicit for ELLs since they may not have mastered the 'meta-language' about their thinking about the topic," writes Jill Kerper Mora of San Diego State University. Keeping this in mind, CLOs should be clear, observable and student-oriented.

CRAFTING A CLO

In terms of actually composing CLOs, there is no common consensus as to the "right" way to go about it. In fact, elements of and approaches to writing CLOs can vary widely from district to district, school to school and teacher to teacher. It is worth cautioning that in any context, consistency and uniformity regarding content language objectives will go far. Whatever method you do choose, aim to streamline CLOs across all grade levels and content areas. This creates a common language- especially around academic language- that serves to guide both teachers and students.

The Newcomer Student includes a series of examples, as well as a strategy for creating your own CLOs. The technique can be used across all grades, subject areas and language ability levels. You'll be surprised by how much this formula simplifies the process of devising appropriate and meaningful content language objectives.

On the following pages, we'll practice writing content-language objectives. Writing CLOs can seem overwhelming at first, but the process becomes more natural with practice. It may be helpful to work in grade-level teams to write, peer review and edit CLOs as a professional development exercise.

The important thing to remember is that each CLO should have five components. In some cases, the *support* element may be left out if: a) no supports are being used; or b) the statement is being simplified as part of learning to write CLOs. Note that the order of the components can and will vary, so as to ensure the clarity of the CLO.

The five critical elements of a CLO are:

- Content
- Domain
- Language function
- Language form
- Language supports

Very briefly, *content* refers to the academic content being taught, according to the standards. *Domain* areas are reading, writing, listening and speaking. *Language function* illustrates the purpose of the language and usually refers back to content. *Language form* defines how language will be used and includes grammar, syntax and vocabulary. *Supports* include resources, tools and modifications that will be available to language learners as they work toward content learning and linguistic expression of that learning.

I advise trying at least one of the following exercises to guide the process of writing effective CLOs. If you have success (or challenges) with these templates, or have a CLO-based resource to share, please consider sharing those with me directly!

A content objective is a standards-driven statement that illustrates what students will be able to know and do as an outcome of a lesson.

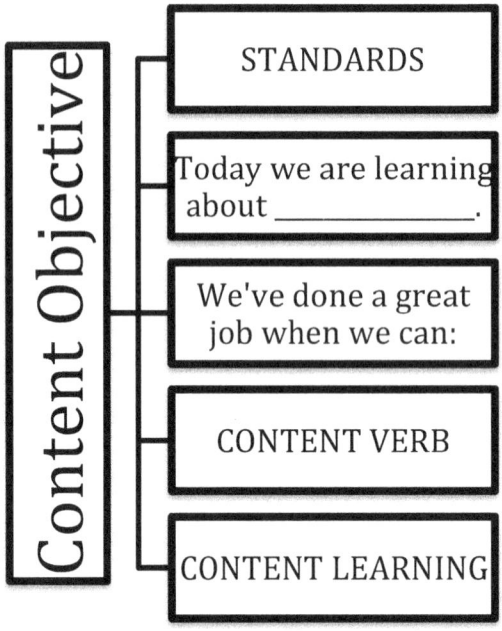

A language objective is a domain-driven statement that defines how students will participate in learning and express understanding of content.

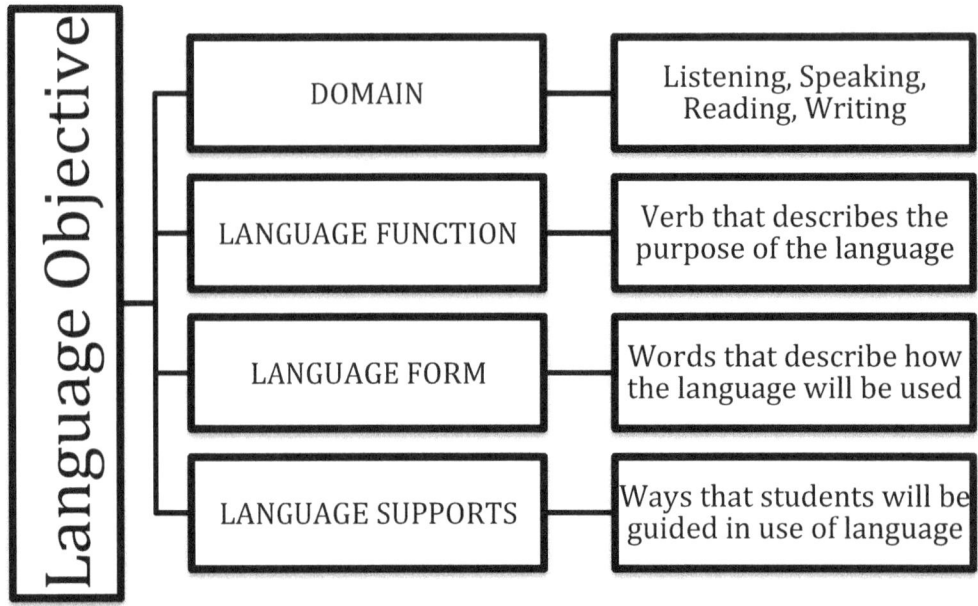

Content and language objectives may be written separately. They can also be merged to create a single statement for learning. In this way, the critical components of each objective are represented in a comprehensive package. The merged value is referred to as a Content Language Objective, or CLO.

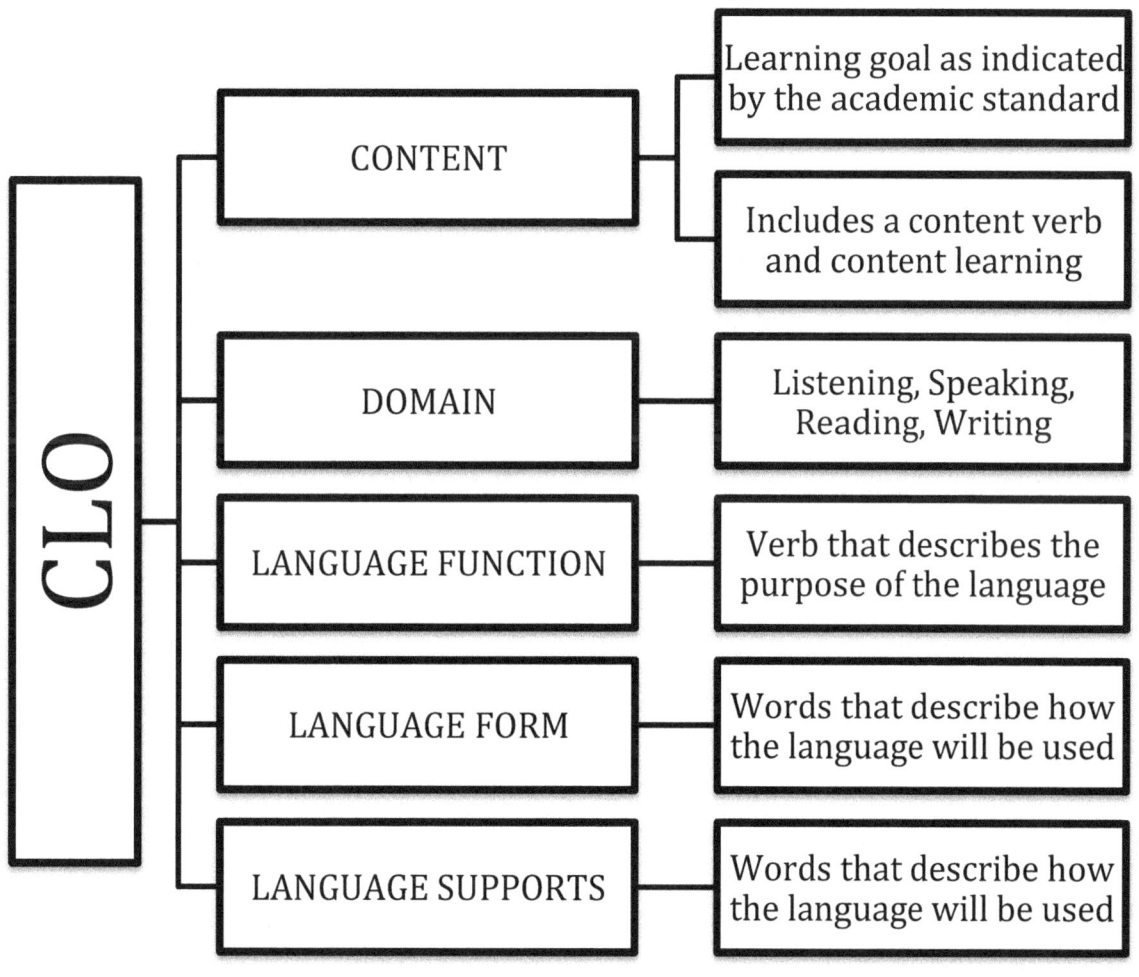

Content Language Objectives Worksheet

1. Content Objective:

What are the standards? What will students learn about?

What will students be expected to do? How will concept understanding be demonstrated?

   a. How will students be expected to produce results? What are the critical thinking or analytical components? (function)

   b. How does the expected output specifically reflect standards? (output)

2. Domain:

What specific language area- listening, speaking, reading, or writing- will students develop and use to express content understanding?

3. Language Function:

How will language be used to develop target domain(s) within the lesson? How will students be expected to communicate?

4. Language Function:

What specific vocabulary, grammar, syntax or sentence structures will be used? (form)

5. Sheltered Supports:

How will students be guided and supported in their learning? How will content and language be made accessible to individual students? What specific tools, instructional techniques or resources will learners employ?

CLO Template 1

We've done a great job when we can:
[domain] <u>language function</u> [OR domain]
--CONTENT-- <u>language form</u> (*SUPPORTS*).

Today we are learning about

_____.

We've done a great job when we can

(d)_____

(function)_____

(c)_____

(form)_____

(s)_____.

Today we are learning about

_____.

We've done a great job when we can

(function)_____

(d)_____

(c)_____

  (form)_____

    (s)_____.

Content Language Objectives Worksheet

Standard: _____	Today we are learning about _____.
Content Objective	We've done a great job when we can: *Content Verb* _____ *Content Learning* _____ _____.
Domain	And we can use our ☐ Listening ☐ Speaking ☐ Reading ☐ Writing skills to
Function *Purpose*	☐Listen for ☐Read ☐Describe ☐Predict ☐Name ☐Summarize ☐Define ☐Label ☐Ask ☐Compare ☐Contrast ☐Explain ☐Use ☐Express ☐State ☐Share ☐Write ☐Revise ☐List ☐Discuss ☐Recite ☐Paraphrase ☐Retell ☐Debate ☐Elaborate ☐Act ☐Compose ☐Persuade ☐Justify ☐Restate ☐Interpret ☐Diagram ☐Respond ☐Narrate ☐Articulate ☐Clarify ☐Identify ☐Other _____ *(what?)* _____ _____
Form *Grammar & Syntax*	Using ☐Nouns ☐Pronouns ☐Verbs ☐Adjectives ☐Adverbs ☐Noun/Verb Agreement ☐Verb Tense ☐Plural endings ☐Proper nouns ☐ Sequence words ☐ If/Then statements ☐Punctuation ☐Possessives ☐Complete sentences ☐Contractions ☐Compound words ☐Compound sentences ☐Synonyms ☐Antonyms ☐"Juicy" words ☐Homonyms ☐Prefixes/Suffixes ☐Other_____
Support	And with the support of ☐ A partner ☐A team ☐A graphic organizer ☐ Visual support ☐A co-operative talk structure ☐ Sentence stems ☐Picture dictionaries ☐Bilingual dictionaries ☐Audio recordings wall ☐ Leveled text ☐Interactive Notebook ☐Manipulatives ☐Picture dictionaries ☐Realia ☐ A buddy/mentor ☐Word wall ☐Technology-based language support ☐ Modeled practice ☐ Building background knowledge ☐Other_____

CLO EXAMPLES:

WRITING: Today we are learning about igneous rocks.
We know we've done a great job when we can investigate the qualities of igneous rocks and we can use our writing skills to record attributes of igneous rocks using correct spelling and with the support of the science word wall. *(content, domain, function, form, support)*

SPEAKING: Today we are learning about subtraction.
We know we've done a great job when we can subtract a single digit number from a double-digit number and we can use our speaking skills to explain our reasoning using complete sentences supported by sentence stems. *(content, domain, function, form, support)*

READING/SPEAKING: Today we are learning about characters.
We know we've done a great job when we can determine the main character of a story and we can use our speaking skills to describe traits of a main character to a partner using descriptive words. *(content, domain, function, support, form)*

LISTENING: Today we are learning about commas and periods.
We know we've done a great job when we can identify commas and periods in a text and we can use our listening skills to interpret the difference between periods and commas in a recording. *(content, domain, function, form, support)*

CLOs- RECEPTIVE & EXPRESSIVE PROCESSING

We can also divide language learning into two fundamental categories: receptive and expressive (also referred to as "productive") processing. Receptive skills are those that deal with intake and understanding of language. Expressive skills refer to language output. One is incoming, the other outgoing; both are necessary for whole language learning.

Of the four modalities of language learning, listening and reading are categorized as receptive skills. When listening or reading, a participant must ingest the information and then process it internally in order to make meaning. Receptive input includes: words, gestures, tone and facial expression. Receptive processing is also referred to as "sponge learning". Newcomers may linger in receptive skill zones as part of the silent period.

Speaking and writing, on the other hand, are expressive qualities and are characterized by some sort of production value. Expressive skills include: letter sounds and pronunciation, vocabulary, semantics, grammar, proper sequencing and the linking of speech to appropriate gestures and facial expressions. Expressive language skills require both receptive exposure and ongoing opportunities for practice in order to fully develop.

Receptive INPUT	Expressive OUTPUT
Listening Reading	Speaking Writing

Receptive & Expressive Verbs for CLOs

Receptive   Expressive

Listening	Reading	Speaking	Writing
Listen	Read	Name	Plan & Evaluate
Distinguish	Read aloud	Identify	Brainstorm
Identify	Infer	Pronounce	Ask/answer
Match	Predict	Respond	Express
Label	Connect	Tell	Explain
Decide	Identify	Ask/Answer	Debate
Assess	Explore	Explain	Illustrate
Connect	Distinguish	Debate	Revise
Select	Locate	List	Rewrite
Choose	Preview	Dictate	List
Copy	Decide	Recall	Classify
Follow directions	Assess	Restate	Create
Act	Summarize	Rephrase	Edit
Arrange	Match	Repeat	Journal
Categorize	Classify	Dramatize	Record
Duplicate	Arrange	Describe	Justify
Point	Select	Justify	Organize
Recognize	Compare	Converse	Opinion
Order	Contrast	Share	Compose
Paraphrase	Discover	Express	Spell
Show	Interpret	Agree/Disagree	Support
Assemble	Map	Summarize	Compare
	Paraphrase	Discuss	Contrast
	Skim	Report	Record
		Paraphrase	Underline
		Give examples	Review
		Negotiate	Report
			Draw
			Create
			Map
			Outline
			Describe
			Evaluate
			Give examples

III: Language Rich Learning Environments

Language rich environments promote direct interaction with contextual print and vocabulary in facilitative, non-threatening ways. These types of learning environments are especially critical for ELLs, who are likely to have had limited exposure to literacy in the new language. Classrooms can and should be designed to promote literacy accessibility across all language and reading levels. Print rich environments accomplish this by providing students many different opportunities to engage in many different components of language and literacy.

The key in creating an effective print-rich environment is to first evaluate the specific ages, interests and learning needs of a student population. An 8th grade Newcomer classroom should not reflect the learning or interest needs of an kindergarten Newcomer classroom, a 3rd grade mainstream classroom or a sophomore Geography class. Print-rich planning should encourage rigorous, grade-level content learning by making language more accessible to developing readers and language learners.

The good news: creating a language rich learning environment is not rocket science. In fact, you are likely incorporating many literacy-promoting techniques in your school or classroom *right now*. Our aim, then, is to grow and refine our repertoire. The following ideas can be employed across multiple grade and content levels. Start with two or three; add on as the school year progresses.

TRAITS OF A LANGUAGE RICH CLASSROOM

- **Rebus Labeling:** Familiar items (door, bookshelf, glue) should be clearly labeled and in student view. Labeling works best when combined with an image. To avoid over-stimulation, refrain from labeling every item in the room. For example, one *"window"* tag/rebus is sufficient, even if there are four windows in the room.

- **Content Language Objectives:** CLOs should be visible at child-height, clearly printed and worded in student-friendly ways. Objectives should be read aloud and together with students at the beginning of each lesson and revisited throughout. Eventually, academic frames used in Content Language Objectives will become predictable, and individual or small groups of students may have the responsibility of reading CLOs aloud to the class.

- **Student-created books:** Learners develop special relationships with stories and books they create. The act of physically and mentally composing text makes it relatable and "readable" in subsequent visits to the material, even if a child is not yet actually (or fully) literate in the text language. Student-created books also encourage sequencing and oral production and fluency, when shared aloud.

- **Teacher-created books:** Teacher-created books serve many of the same functions and advantages of student-created texts. Instructor-created books, however, are more deliberate in their use of content-based vocabulary, target sight words and proper grammar and punctuation.

- **Name Labels:** Students love seeing their name- it's also a great way to encourage print concepts! Options: label student photos, desks, lockers, cubbies, notebooks, attendance markers

- **Displayed Co-Created Work:** These samples should remain in student view for the day or days for which they are relevant. Ideas include: morning message, whole group text summaries, co-created objectives, and daily weather or "news" reports.

- **Print-based charts:** Essential charts are very helpful. Again, the caution is in not overdoing it. Too many posters create clutter and issues with over-stimulation. Pick and choose carefully, and re-adjust as students' specific learning and unit needs change. Examples: days of the week, months of the year, weather, colors, sight words, planets, homonyms, life cycle, Pledge of Allegiance
    - Alphabet, calendars, schedules, directions, number line, teacher helpers, anchor charts and rubrics are posted in clear student view and referred to often.

- **Frequent Read-Alouds:** Listening to teacher read-alouds and audio read-alouds of text encourage auditory processing and help students learn to identify and use appropriate intonation and emphasis. Tip: Read like an adult. Learners should hear (and learn to mimic) natural tonal fluctuation.

- **Language based Technology and Media:** Computer-based programs that support language learning and literacy can be incorporated as station work. Watch for: computer use as a crutch, diversion or means of "occupying" a learner during mainstream instruction.

- **Displayed student work:** This is a very powerful tool for promoting student confidence and encouraging learners to read and reflect on peer accomplishments. Posted teacher celebrations on the work (or peer celebrations) also encourage reading!

- **Writing Centers:** Writing centers are a chance for students to explore print and practice skills in differentiated ways. Provide different sized writing tools to develop fine motor skills and interesting paper sources that invite participation. Suggestions: shopping lists, thank-you cards, Pen Pal writing, journaling, invitations, notes to teachers and school personnel, postcards, reading response logs. Early writers will benefit from sentence stems and graphic organizer choices.

- **Teacher-print:** Teacher-printed dictation, summaries of student expression, daily vocabulary or other relevant items are meaningful to students as models for appropriate spelling, spacing, punctuation and print.

- **Murals:** Whole class murals invite students to contribute understanding and insight on a theme in ways that are accessible to each at his or her own language development level. A mural on the story, *Swimmy,* by Leo Lionni, for example, might include a story line or multiple story lines; labeled pictures of fish, characters with thinking or speaking bubbles; pictures or descriptions of the environment; single or multi-sentence structures about the story; opinions on characters or plot; or non-fiction statements about fish. A word of note: language development is key. That is, while illustration is an important element of mural work, it should not be the only element. Encourage students to exchange topic-focused thoughts with their peers as they work and to include some variation of print expression with every illustration.

- **Classroom Libraries:** Inviting, comfortable classroom libraries are an essential component of the Newcomer classroom (or any classroom!). Exemplary classroom libraries are age, ability and interest appropriate, and are inclusive of a global community. Newcomer classrooms are especially diverse and include an incredible range of reading and interest levels; libraries should reflect this diversity. Books should be organized and clearly labeled. Students will benefit from reading books at their level and also exploring other texts in interest areas that are outside of reader ability. Early readers, especially, will learn to explore print concepts, picture cues,

captions, directionality and broad content idea shaping. Depending on the age and grade level, Newcomer classroom libraries areas should include:
- Picture, English and dual language (where applicable) dictionaries
- Tactile and Predictable Picture Books
- Special-interest books
- Multi-cultural books
- Dual-language books, where accessible
- Grade-level content texts with supports
- Maps and atlases
- Magazines
- Play-based and life-based print: magnetic letters, menus, phone books, recipes, bus schedules, business cards

- **Word Walls:** The teaching community has many thoughts and ideas on word walls. Alphabetically, by unit, by tiers, by reading group, by color code? Growing throughout the year or rotating through? So many choices! The bottom line is that word walls work! Ask around, try different variations… see what works best for you, then modify and refine.

- **Theme displays:** Theme displays are helpful in anchoring ideas related to an ongoing unit. These are excellent areas to post unit vocabulary, charts, pictures, student work and teacher dictation related to a topic.

- **Involve parents:** This may be the most important trait of all. Most Newcomer parents *do* wish to help their students learn English and succeed in school. In the vast majority of cases, Newcomer parents are eager to take part in their child's successes and are open to guidance from the teacher and school. So- make this process fun! Allow for activities that can be completed as a family. Host parents at the school to discuss cultural expectations around parent involvement in learning and creating quiet "homework" spaces at home. Invite parents to share their strengths with students. Consider posting parent notes of encouragement to students in the classroom (heritage language is fine!). Parents can gain confidence by working with their children on math, teaching them the history of their heritage country, creating regional maps, or explaining in-depth science concepts in the native language. Learning is a collaborative process- and parents are an essential link!

Exposing children to more than one form of communication sparks interest and interest turns into learning. This connection quickly becomes the making of meaning for reading.

–Leyva & McClure, et al

Language-Functional Environment Survey

TEAM MEMBER	
ROOM	DATE
ROLE	

	1	2	3	4	5	6
Content Language Objectives		Notes:				
Alphabet						
Number line						
Calendar						
Schedule						
Rebus Labeling						
Student Names						
Word Wall						
Desk Labels						
Teacher print						
Posted Student work						
Co-created work						
Theme displays						
Murals						
Maps						
Print-based charts						
Anchor Charts						
Cultural Items						
Graphic Organizers						
Sentence Stems						
Picture Dictionaries						
Student Created Books						
Read Aloud Observed						
Language Based Technology						
Stations/Centers						
Grouped Seating						
Student Library						

SIGNATURE _____

© The Newcomer Fieldbook, 2017

IV: Lesson Planning for Newcomer ELLs

Of all of the concerns or frustrations that teachers share with me, one takes the cake. Here's the scenario:

A Newcomer teacher receives a grade level curriculum set. He is determined to achieve all parts of the curriculum and vows to follow the course with fidelity. Yet, no matter how hard he tries, his pace trails the mainstream classes; his students are still working through the second unit, even as the next-door class is testing out of Unit 3. There is vocabulary everywhere. Each day, he presents his students with new sets of words. Many of his students are still absorbing basic English commands. Yet, Mr. Teacher is determined to continue, par for the course.

Each "day" in the teacher's guide is equivalent to the feat of scaling a mountain with a hundred pound pack in bare feet. In ninety minutes, he aims to cover adjectives, main idea, choral reading and small groups, as prescribed.

The further Mr. Teacher lags behind in the manual, the more overwhelmed he feels. The students seem to be learning a little bit of a lot of things, but mastering only a very few. Day after day, the team goes through the motions, falling further and further behind, feeling more and more defeated.

Enough!

Of course, I am not advocating that any teacher throw his or her teacher's manual out of the window. We *do* have a duty to adhere to our school's curriculum, and certainly to the standards. However, in many cases, it is wise and healthy to allow for some wiggle-room. In other words, when teachers and students are overwhelmed, learning ceases. We can enhance productivity on all ends when we concentrate our efforts on the most essential elements of the curriculum. This is especially true in Newcomer classrooms, where it can be even easier to miss the forest for the trees.

When I sit with teachers to look through their lesson guides, we look for the most essential elements of a unit or a lesson. What *must* the students gain from this period of time? What does student success in this unit look like? Why is that success important? What will we build on top of it? How can I be more purposeful in my planning?

I use the following graphic organizers to help facilitate this paring-down process. Keep in mind that some students *will* be prepared to access and engage in most or all components of a lesson/unit. Fantastic! Let them go! Or, work through this type of content as a station or small group activity.

In looking at the big picture, I offer one piece of advice: simplify, simplify, simplify!

Newcomer "Bare Bones" Planning

Foundation	**1. Standard(s):** _____ _____ **2. Content Language Objective:** Today we are learning about_____. We've done a great job when we can _____ _____ and we can use our _____ skills to _____ using_____ and with the support of_____.
Background	**3. English Proficiency Levels:** _____ _____ _____ _____ **4. Goals:** Before this lesson, students will: _____ _____ After this lesson, students will: _____ _____

Lesson Body	These parts of the scripted lesson will help my students reach the end goal: _____ _____ _____ These parts of the scripted lesson will better serve my students on another day/ in another lesson: _____ _____ _____ This vocabulary is essential: This vocabulary is for another day: Content will be made more digestible by supplementing with *this* key support(s). _____ Students will lead their learning by _____
Assessment	My students will demonstrate understanding when they _____ _____ I will provide feedback to my students by _____ _____

EL YAAFOURI

Lesson:_____

Main Idea/Most Important Take-Away

Not the Main Idea, but critical right now

Not the Main Idea, and not critical right now

© The Newcomer Teacher

V: Sheltered Instruction Techniques

Effective Newcomer teaching systems are structured with the principles of sheltered instruction in mind. These techniques are not components of an exclusive program or curriculum. Rather, they are tools for teaching and learning that can be applied to and incorporated into any existing program to explicitly promote language development.

Sheltered, or scaffolded, instructional practices are platforms from which language learners can engage in rigorous content investigation. In this way, students are able to access and demonstrate essential knowledge through modified systems of learning, without compromising the integrity of the lesson itself.

Strategies that are associated with sheltered instruction foster academically focused student talk, intra/interdependent problem solving skills, effective collaboration and healthy cross-cultural communication skill development. These practices benefit Newcomer and non-Newcomers alike and support learners across a range of language and skill levels.

Sheltered education encompasses a range of instructional techniques aimed at guiding and directing language learners toward proficiency, within an environment that endorses safety and facilitated risk-taking. At the crux of impactful scaffolded instruction are effective language learning objectives, which can be incorporated into every subject, each day. These cornerstones provide a powerful sense of directionality for both the educator and the learner and fuel a focused sense of productivity.

Sheltered instruction is a manifestation of the Comprehension Hypothesis for language learning. The Comprehension Hypothesis is rooted in the idea that, "we acquire language when we understand messages containing aspects of language that we have not acquired, but are developmentally ready to acquire." (Krashen, 2013). That is, language learning best occurs in natural settings, drawing holistically from what we hear and read. It develops via exposure to comprehensible input, or bite-sized digestible pieces of language understanding.

This is in direct contrast to the *skill-building theory*, which presses for direct, rote learning of grammar, vocabulary and spelling knowledge. Briefly, skill-building strategies are conscious measures, while comprehension-based learning is subconscious and indirect. Research overwhelmingly indicates that language learning is enhanced and accelerated when Comprehension Hypothesis methods are applied. In fact, evidence shows that,

> "Students in beginning-level second language classes based on the Comprehension Hypothesis consistently outperform students in classes based on skill-building tests of communication, and do at least as well as, and often slightly better than, students in skills-based classes on tests of grammar." (Krashen, 2003)

Sheltered instruction is directly representative of Comprehension Hypothesis ideals. Its primary goal is to provide language learners with a comprehensible input through the implementation of specific instructional tools and practices. Sheltered instruction is critical in the context of Newcomer instruction in that it focuses on *content* over language.

When students are exposed to content knowledge in comprehensible ways, appropriate language output is a holistic byproduct. Additionally, anxiety and pressure to learn the new language may be significantly diffused in sheltered subject matter settings. In fact, "Students in sheltered subject matter classes acquire as much language or more language than students in traditional [ESL-direct] classes and also learn impressive amounts of subject matter". (Krashen, 2013, 1991; Dupuy, 2000)

Basic elements of sheltered instruction include: pacing; modified speech; routine and predictability; use of visuals, realia and manipulatives; or explicitly introduced body language, gestures and facial cues. Sentence stems, graphic organizers (such as Frayer models, Venn Diagrams or word-mapping), co-operative talk structures (Insider-outside circles, fishbowls, numbered heads) are examples of strategies and tools associated with sheltered instruction. SIOP lesson planning, or "Sheltered Instruction Observation Protocol" (Echevarria & Short), is frequently implemented as part of sheltered-instruction instruction.

When we integrate sheltered techniques into existing curricula and classroom protocol, we invite Newcomer students to participate in learning in meaningful, constructive ways. We also support team building and interpersonal skills. These rudiments are indispensible to healthy social integration for heritage culture individuals. Similarly, explicitly facilitated cooperative interaction is critical in disseminating cultural tolerance, understanding and acceptance on the part of host-culture students, a key indicator for positive school climate.

Additional, detailed information on Sheltered Instruction techniques, see **The Newcomer Student: An Educator's Guide to Aid Transition,** *Chapters 6-8*

Sheltered Co-operative Activity Starters

Note: Sentence stems for all activities are highly recommended.

Think-Pair-Share/Think-Pair-Write: Students share thoughts with a partner; switch roles; and share out (or write).	Inside-Outside Circle: One group forms inner circle; second group forms circle around first, facing a partner; facilitator calls one circle to respond to a prompt; outside circle shifts one spot to the right.	Numbered Heads: Number students in a group 1-4; call out a prompt; all groups discuss; at random, call out a number; that person from each group reports out team's response.
Line-Ups: Form a line on the floor with tape; assign a scale to the line (e.g. 1-10); students move to spots on a line that aligns with the degree to which they agree/disagree with a prompt.	Corners: Assign four corners these values: *agree, disagree, strongly agree, strongly disagree*; students move to corner that aligns with the degree to which they agree/disagree with a prompt.	Jigsaw: Students read and or/research different parts of a text; in small groups, each member shares out critical information, or "teaches" his or her text.
Popsicle Sticks: Members of a group receive popsicle sticks. As part of a group discussion, members must use all of their sticks, but must stop talking when all sticks are used.	Fishbowl: One cooperative team sits inside a larger group circle and discusses a topic; outside circle listens and/or records thoughts; whole group discussion and/or independent writing follows.	Graffiti: Form small cooperative groups; assign each group a topic and a large poster; students record thoughts/illustrations about topic; after a time, papers rotate; continue until posters return to home groups.

Gallery Walk: Student samples are posted around room; students walk to observe/ take notes/comment on peer work samples.	Three Part Interview: In partners groups, one student responds to a prompt while the other listens; partners reverse roles; partners share out, write about responses or join another partner group to report on discussions.	Rally Table: Students are arranges in small groups; teacher issues a prompt or category; students work together to brainstorm and record as many correct responses to the prompt as possible.
Mix & Match: Half of students are issued cards with questions; the other students will have cards with appropriate responses to questions; matching pairs must find each other.	Merry-Go-Round: Hang posters related to specific topics/questions around room; in small groups, students brainstorm at a poster; students rotate until all groups reach all posters.	Listen-Retell: In pairs, one partner speaks; the other students rephrases his or her partner's words (advanced- also adds on a relevant phrase or thought); reverse.
Draw It (Kagan): Students sit back to back; one partner describes a noun or concept without saying the actual word; the other partner interprets the description as a drawing; partners discuss and switch.	Machine: Students are given a prompt; one at a time, students add to "class machine" by connecting to machine and contributing a movement and/or sound that lends itself to the prompt.	Stray: In small group discussion settings, teacher occasionally calls out "Stray!" one person from each group moves to another team and shares; discussions continue. ("Strays" can also be released in multiples.)

(Think-Pair-Share, Inside-Outside Circle, Corners, Mix & Match, Numbered Heads, Rally Table, Draw it, Strays: *credit Kagan, 1998*)

11 LEARNING FROM THE EXPERTS: THE VOICES OF EXITED NEWCOMER ELLS

This is it. The final chapter. And I want nothing to do with it. In fact, I'm so excited to turn this time over to some of the best imaginable teachers- our students.

Messages From Our Students

This is it. The final chapter. And I want nothing to do with it. In fact, I'm so excited to turn this time over to some of the best imaginable teachers- our students.

Throughout the course of my teaching career, I've often wondered- what will my students say about all of this one day? How do they perceive my instruction and our curriculum? What would they tell me if they had the full English expression to do so?

I am also very aware of the fact that our students' voices are noticeably absent from our professional development agendas. Why is this so? Aren't our students among our most valuable teaching resources? Then why is student input so overlooked in our attempts to develop curriculum and train teachers?

As I've been fortunate to watch my former students grow from young children into young adults, I've had the opportunity to encourage some very honest conversation about students' perspectives of Newcomer protocol. Of course, each student represents a snapshot in time- of specific policy in place, of the degree of teaching experience at that time, of the tools and resources available in that school year, and of the overall picture of health of a school at a given time.

The responses are also wholly subjective. To me, that's the beauty of it. Education cannot be a wholly standardized affair (despite certain institutional efforts to make it so). Learning, by its very nature, must be static, fluid, adjustable, and expandable. To the same end, our subjects are dynamic entities. Students absorb, digest, process, invent and reinvent ideas through incredibly unique filters. How would or could we expect a standardized output?

I'm happy to end this text with some very non-uniform insights in the form of blatant student honesty.

Here's what I wanted to know:
- What were the key "take-aways" for students as participants in Newcomer-ESL programming?
- What worked for them? What didn't?
- What do students wish that I (or other practitioners) could have known about them, but that was difficult for them to express in English (or that they felt uncomfortable communicating with a teacher about)?
- What specific tools, resources or experiences made learning English easier?
- What would students recommend that I (or other practitioners) do differently to better facilitate language learning?

As part of the student insight piece, ELLs from all over the world, ages 7 to 70 took part in a twelve-question survey about their experiences. The responses are telling of our own work as educators. The narratives are at once heart breaking and uplifting. These are the voices of our ELLs, as humans, as learners, as individuals who are ready to make a positive mark on the world around them.

LET'S MEET OUR PANEL:

Samir Mongar, age 12. Heritage: Bhutanese. Arrived in U.S. at age 8 from the Domajapa refugee camp in Nepal. First languages: British Sign Language, Nepali, American Sign Language. Other: Male, Hindi

Jemima Safi, age 14. Heritage: Congolese. Arrived in U.S. at age 11 from the Democratic Republic of Congo. First languages: French, Lingala, Swahili.

Lamyia Adhab, age 9. Heritage: Iraqi. Arrived in U.S. at age 7 from Iraq. First languages: Arabic. Other: Female, Muslim

Obed Kende, age 11. Heritage: Gabonese. Arrived in U.S. at age 6 from Gabon. First Languages: French. Other languages: local tribal language. Other: Male,

Karla, age 11. Heritage: Guatemalan. Arrived in U.S. at age 9 from Guatemala. First language: Spanish.

Gadson John Mazimbi Woodard, age 10. Heritage: Congolese and Malawian. Arrived in U.S. at age 6 from Malawi. First languages: French. Other: Male, Christian

Francisco Lozano, age 70. Heritage: Mexican. Arrived in U.S. at age 5. First language: Spanish, Portugese. Other: Male, Roman Catholic, husband, father, grandfather.

Fahad, Age 9. Heritage: Iraqi. Arrived in U.S. at age 6. First language: Arabic. Other: Male, Christian.

Elvina, Age 27. Heritage: Ethnic Karen (Myanmar Burma). Arrived in U.S. at age 18 from Thailand. First language: Karen,

Babak Khoshnevisan, age 34. Heritage: Iranian. Arrived in U.S. at age 31. First languages: Farsi, Arabic, French. Other: Male, Muslim/Christian

Zar Hin Oo, age 9. Heritage: Burmese. Arrived in U.S. at age 5 from Thailand. First language: Burmese. Other: Female, Muslim

Yari Sissoko, age 12. Heritage: Malian. Yari was born in the U.S. and returned to Mali as a toddler. She came back to America again at age 8, from Mali. First languages: Bambara, French. Other: female, Muslim.

Leela Timsina, age 40. Heritage: Bhutanese. Arrived in U.S. at age 33 from Nepal. First languages: Nepali is my first language. I speak other two languages fluently. Other: Male, Hindi.

Birtukan Girmay, age 14. Heritage: Sudanese. Arrived in U.S. at age 7 from Eritrea. First languages: Tigrinya, Amharic, Arabic. Other: female.

Jor Roon, age 14. Heritage: Mon Burmese. Arrived in U.S. at age 3 from Thailand. First languages, Mon, Burmese. Other: Male, Buddhist.

Anonymous 1 (AN-Chile), age 38. Heritage: Chilean. Arrived in U.S. at 23. First languages: Spanish. Other: Male, Catholic

Anonymous 2 (AN-Bhutan), age 20. Heritage: Bhutanese. Arrived in U.S. at age 12 from a refugee camp in Nepal. First languages: Nepali. I also speak Hindi fluently, and currently learning Spanish. Other: Hindu, Female

What do you remember most about your first day of school in the U.S.?

- I was happy to finally meet a lot of new people. I love meeting people. –Samir
- On the first day of school, I really didn't want to go. I came with my twin brother, Seth, and we were in the same class. My dad would sing to me, "Try, try" in French. I didn't want to come at all. But then, after I started coming, I was really glad I was in school. My teacher was very nice and there was a helper, she was Asian and she was learning English, too. That made me feel better. My teacher was very funny and let us play games sometimes. –Obed
- Confused, lost, and feeling of illusion. –Leela
- It was really hard for me to understand anybody. It was really confusing. –Karla
- I didn't understand what anyone was saying. Everyone looked so different. -Jor
- I was a little shy. I didn't know where to go. The school was really big and I didn't know the language and I didn't have any friends yet. It was a lot of new things. -Birtukan
- The hot sun, traffic noises, smelly bus, sky scrapers, unfamiliar faces, the noise of the AC running in a tiny classroom, [feeling] very scared and uncomfortable. It was hard trying to understand the lesson, but it was harder trying to understand my classmates

during classroom activities due to our different accents. I felt like I was in a movie. It was beautiful and I felt very adventurous. Everything was new and strange. The elevator, vending machines, ramen noodles and coffee aroma, all in a closed painted room filled with chemicals. I longed for open space, clear air and the noise of jungle. -Elvina

- It was frustrating and I was flabbergasted by the way they teach here in the US. Back home the teacher is the sage. Here, the teacher acts like a ghost in the wind. Everything is different. -Babak
- Scary. I was [placed] into a class where I was learning too many things at the same time. I wish they taught us language for the first month before we were taught other subjects. (AN-Bhutan)
- It was totally different [than school in Chile] and very relaxed. –AN 1
- I remember feeling LOST. There was no bilingual education in the St. Louis Public Schools in 1951. It was sink or swim from Day One of Kindergarten. –Fransico
- People came to help me. The principal and the vice principal both came to help me. -Zar
- I was really nervous. -Fahad
- I remember how afraid I was because I didn't know any English and thought I would never be like the other kids. –Jemima
- I remember that I was not a very happy person when I first came to to America. I did not know anybody in my school or in town. I didn't speak any English or type or write. I didn't even know how to read. I only knew two words in English: "no" and "yes". So, if you asked me what my name was, I would reply, "No" or "Yes"! I also remember when I met my friends and my teacher, Ms. Stash. –Gadson

How did you find U.S. school to be different from schooling in other countries where you went to school?

- I love that teachers in the U.S. care and are willing to learn new things even from the students. I love that U.S. teachers have conversations with us not lecturing. –Elvina
- The schools in the U.S. lacked discipline. -Jor
- In Iraq, we didn't have busses. Everyone had to walk to school. Also, you have to pay to go to school there. My mom didn't have enough money, so I didn't go to school. Some kids went, but it was very dangerous to walk. Mostly you had to sneak out very carefully to go to school. Here, kids go to school and they don't worry about it. – Lamyia
- U.S. schools are practical based where as back home schools were theoretical. Full of resources vs. scarcity of very important topic too. –Leela
- Schooling in the U.S. was different because my teachers' intentions were different in the two countries. In Mali, my teachers wanted good grades. Here, my new teacher wanted success. Also, in Mali we only use cursive writing. When I got to third grade

in America, nobody was writing in cursive and I hadn't learned regular print. Sometimes I had trouble sharing my writing with other students! -Yari

- Here you don't have to remember anything because we have technology for everything. People bully each other a lot here. Teaching style is different. When I was back home, student stayed in the class and teachers moved to different classes to teach. –AN- Bhutan
- We always have two schools. One school is for math and language. The other school is for Burmese Muslim. That's where we learn about our religion and Burma. I go to two schools like that in America, too. First, I go to regular school. Then, when I get home I go to the Burmese school by our apartments. -Zar
- I think the U.S. schools are very nice. When I was in Africa, I never really liked my school. My teacher would hit or whip me when I did anything wrong- even though it was usually my little cousin who got me in trouble! –Gadson
- I wasn't experienced in going to school with a teacher who spoke English. It's a lot different in my country. There, if you don't listen, you are punished. Also, in my country we didn't have any homework. You do all of your learning at school. I had to learn what to do with homework. -Birtukan
- School in Iraq is a lot harder. We don't get very long breaks or summers and we have a LOT more homework. We also don't have a lot of recess time like we do here. -Fahad
- What I remember about the first day is that they didn't give us homework. We didn't get homework the whole week! In Nepal, it doesn't matter if it's the first day of school or the last day of school, you *will* have homework. And they really beat you at the school if you don't bring your homework. So, when I told my parents we didn't have homework in America, they wouldn't believe me! -Samir
- I didn't go to school in another country until I did an MA in Mexico at the age of 40. – Francisco
- Schooling in the US is interspersed with the use of technology and it seems that without emerging technology you fail to pass. Schools are technology-oriented. Courses are student fronted and you can always negotiate. -Babar
- Here teachers give you the option to think, ask for your opinion, make mistakes and learn. Back home just memorize books. –AN1
- It is a different language here and the standards in Congo are super different from the standards here. -Jemima
- School is a lot harder in Guatemala. I feel like the things they teach you in first grade in Guatemala are the things they teach you in third or fourth grade here. The teachers are harder, too. A lot harder. There, the teachers can hit you if you talk too much or you forget your homework. Here, they say, "It's ok, don't do it next time." -Karla
- I remember using the computers a lot in America. I'd never used a computer before. We also had a lot of free time, and time to sleep at school. Nobody sleeps at school in Gabon. Also, in America we eat at school. In Gabon, the kids go home to eat and then come back. –Obed

What is something you wish your first teacher in America knew about you (but you didn't have enough English to tell them)?

- The first thing I really wanted my teacher to know was that I didn't like being alone. The second thing was that I was very emotional and I still am. I cry when I do something wrong and I always think that I am in trouble. -Gadson
- I wish she was more playful. I wish she knew that I'm actually playful. –Lamyia
- I am Muslim. I am a special kid. I go to two schools. That's why it's sometimes hard to do my homework for regular school. -Zar
- Yeah! I am great at statistics. However, the idiomatic language of the teacher made it hard for me to catch up. I felt baaaad. –Babak
- I didn't know any English and it was hard for me to communicate. I wanted my teacher to know that when I started learning more English I was like a translator for everything. I don't have brothers or sisters. It's just me and my mom. My mom got sick a LOT in our country and in America. I took care of her. In America, I had to be the translator for the doctors and everyone. Now she's doing better. She has a job here now, so that's really good. -Birtukan
- Make sure that your (teacher) asks questions to check if the students understand. Give new students an opportunity to openly share their ideas. Create such a platform that newcomers could come and be assets. -Leela
- I might not understand English well, but I speak three other languages and I had Associates degree in teaching, so I am not unintelligent. I know a lot of stuff, I just didn't know English language. –Elvina
- I wish she knew that even if I didn't understand she would clarify and I didn't need to ask any questions. -Yari
- She was so ignorant. Without knowing anything about me she made an assumption that I came to America to learn English. I DID NOT come America to learn English; we were refugees. I didn't tell her anything because she didn't wanted to hear what MY experience was. –AN-Bhutan
- I was trying my best to understand them. They needed to be patient with me. -Jor
- That I shouldn't be held back. In my country I already did second grade. I already knew the things in second grade. But In America they said that because of my birthday I would be in first grade. I kind of did the work for one grade, but then had to do it again because of my birthday. It made me upset. -Fahad
- I wish my first teacher in America knew that she could call me Gaby. On the computer, it always said Karla Gabriella. Karla came from my grandpa's name, Karl. But my grandma started calling me Gaby. I wanted other people to call me Gaby because I miss my grandma and I can't see her anymore. -Karla
- I was too scared to tell a teacher on the playground that I wanted to play with the big kids, because in Gabon I always played with my big brothers and their friends, so I liked playing with the big kids more. On our playground, we were only allowed to

play with other kindergartners. –Obed
- I wish she knew that I'm a fast learner and I love challenges. –Jemima
- Thank you, Mrs. Mary Claus -- not for your world-famous spelling textbooks, but for helping a monolingual little Mexican boy take his first steps in English in your 1952 first grade at Clark Elementary. Thank you for using your pedagogical skills and your common sense to engage me in projects and day-to-day learning tasks -- in spite of no training in working with ELLs. I now realize that you were using a combination of sight reading plus phonetics. I do wish you had been aware that I wanted to be more involved in more activities. I now know you realized I wasn't ready for some types of participation. Oh, and thank you for stopping the Korean War air raid drills when we started crying. What with my almost nonexistent English and the sound effects record you were forced to use, I really didn't know what was going on. I was terrified! -Francisco

What is something you wish other students in America knew about you (but maybe you didn't have enough English to tell them)?

- I wish my friends here knew that I had three really good friends in Iraq. They were all like me. Our families knew each other. We did everything together. –Lamyia
- I am just like them. My immigration status does not define me. -Jor
- I truly appreciated the way my classmates made me feel part of the class. I would also like to thank them for helping the teacher make sure I understood the tasks we had to carry out. -Francisco
- I wish they knew more about my cultural background before judging me. –AN-Bhutan
- I wish they knew that if you start out with a good teacher you can succeed. I also had a very lucky beginning with parents that pushed me to learn. -Yari
- I wish they knew that just because I am from a different place, I am still a human and they didn't have to treat me in an inhumane way. –Jemima
- That I don't have any brothers or sisters. It made it harder because I was alone a lot. -Birtukan
- I wanted my classmates to know that I wanted them to be my friends. I wanted them to appreciate that I liked and believed different things than them. I wanted them to like me just the way I am. –Gadson
- I wanted them to know that I don't want to get bullied. I didn't want them to be mean to me. -Zar
- I sounded very rude and disrespectful, Just because I didn't speak English, understand this foreign language, and unfamiliar with this culture, so I didn't know better. I wasn't ignorant and rude. -Elvina
- That all Spanish speakers are not just Mexicans...there are more countries in the world that speak Spanish. –AN1

- Make sure to share that student has lots of potential but little English. It doesn't mean that a student who has less English doesn't have any knowledge. –Leela
- That I am from a particular region with a particular religion or skin color does not mean I am a terrorist. They did not show good behavior at first. Now, we are all friends. -Babak

What were your biggest thoughts or worries about going to school in America?

- I just remember being so nervous. Even though I was seven, I'd never been to school before. I didn't know what it would be like. –Lamyia
- I thought it would be hard and I was very nervous. Especially because I didn't know English. –Karla
- I was worried that I would do or say something wrong and offend people, so I kept everything to myself, and being as quiet as I could be. -Elvina
- Bullies. They made my middle school experience kind of a hell. –AN-Bhutan
- My worry was that my friends would not like me for who I am. –Gadson
- My biggest worry was how to seek help against the bullies (older kids) who made my life miserable. I remember not having enough English to ask for help. –Francisco
- My biggest worries were: How was I going to remember a language I hadn't spoken in years? Also, I worried that I was going to be different. -Yari
- The language problem. –Leela
- I was worried that no one would be my friend because I was Muslim. I was worried that my teachers would hit me, because they can do that in my country. Also, I didn't know how to go anywhere. -Zar
- That people would bully me. I was bullied a lot when I went to school in Eritrea, so I thought people would bully me here, too. -Birtukan
- I had no idea about how to manage my studies. I did not know what are the requirements and I failed to accomplish some assignments. –Babak
- I was scared I wouldn't understand the subjects they taught me. -Jor
- My biggest worries were that I would never make friends that liked me and that I would get bullied. –Jemima
- No worries at all ..... oh! I guess money was my biggest worry. –AN1

What is something that your first teacher or teachers did that made you feel safe and welcomed?

- My Kindergarten and first grade teachers made me feel welcome. They were very patient and made sure I understood what was expected of me. My classmates also got me to take part in play activities during recess. -Francisco
- She helped me feel better because she got other students to translate things for me into Spanish. Then, at least I could understand what was happening. –Karla
- She told me that I could learn English because it isn't hard and that I will become very successful in life. –Jemima
- My teacher saw that I didn't have a lot of clothes and that me and my mom didn't have any coats. She came to our house with coats and clothes and a lot of food. That was really helpful. My mom was so grateful. -Birtukan
- Constructive feedback back with teaching resources. -Leela
- They helped me not only with lessons but also culturally. I was having a hard time finding an apartment without credit and they helped me. I appreciate them. -Babak
- I would help my teacher translate for other kids. Then I felt proud, like I had an important job. –Fahad
- We had story time, which was really fun. Also, we got prizes which motivated me to have more [Class Dojo] points and have all my homework in. -Yari
- People welcomed me. My teacher said a lot of nice things. She said that my hijab was beautiful and that I was a smart kid. -Zar
- Asking questions about me, my family and country and listening to me. I appreciate the teacher going above and beyond trying to help me learn and understand her lesson. I can see and feel a caring heart through her eyes and smile. That was very comforting! I felt like everything will be okay even though it's hard to understand and navigate my ways through foreign language because of that smile and a caring heart, I had hope. -Elvina
- My first teacher introduced me to another student who spoke my language. -Jor
- One of my teachers praised me in class about my knowledge and asked me to help other domestic students. –An-Bhutan
- Gadson's mom speaking: We had the opportunity to meet his first teacher the day he enrolled. She immediately got down on his level and spoke to him, making him the center of her attention. She also showed him around the classroom and showed him where he would sit. This took away a lot of anxiety about what school would be like.
- Super polite! Big smile. –AN-Chile

Tell about something in your first years of school in America that was hard for you or made you feel uncomfortable.

- Math was really hard for me. Also, I didn't know English, so it was really hard for me to understand my teacher. –Lamyia
- Many people made fun of me because I was much taller than the other kids. –Jemima
- When a lot of people were talking only in English, it was hard for me because I couldn't understand and I couldn't fit in and I felt left out. It was actually really hard for me. –Karla
- The one thing that bugged me was when everyone kept on talking and playing so that I couldn't learn what the teacher was teaching me. –Gadson
- I often misinterpreted what I read/heard. I could read "fruit cellar" because we read along as the teacher read aloud; however, I thought it meant "fruit seller." The teacher helped me figure it out, but I was mortified. This was in third grade. I can't blame the teacher because I remember I wasn't paying attention to the context, which would have made the meaning clear. -Francisco
- For me, language organizational skills. –Leela
- The way we learned math in Mali was a little different, so I had a little bit of trouble getting used to the way we do math here. -Yari
- I was competing with native speakers and obviously they had a better language and they were impressive. Other than that I never received good writing instruction and everything was writing here. I felt behind. –Babak
- There are not a lot of people I know or that look like me or that are Muslim. English was a little hard for me. -Zar
- Everything in America was new. For example, it was hard for us to go buy food. We didn't know what the money meant. We thought $50 was like a dollar. We didn't know these things yet and I didn't learn it in school until after. -Birtukan
- I took English classes for 2 months then attended Aurora Community College. Just because I didn't know the culture and the language well, I felt like an outsider. I didn't get the jokes, the sarcasm, and I could not participate in common sense conversations such as football, pop culture, music and so on. I felt like I had so much to learn besides education. -Elvina
- It was very difficult. AN-Bhutan
- Many people did not talk to me because I was different. -Jor
- The American college system is totally different. I was confused about the academic curriculum- taking my own classes? It took me time to understand it. –AN-Chile

If you could change something about the way your first teacher in the U.S. taught or the way he or she taught you, what would it be?

- I would ask her to give me a background knowledge of something before discussion, so I wouldn't feel very lost and awkward. Also, I think it would be beneficial to study the culture along with the language, because in order to be able to access the texts, we need to have a background knowledge of this culture. For example, not knowing about baseball when a math problem is based around baseball gives us disadvantages to understanding the math problem.–Elvina
- I wish he would've been a little more patient with me. -Jor
- I would change how she always gave me work that was much easier than the other kids. –Jemima
- I would want her to help me more with reading instead of giving me free time. –Obed
- Start teaching any lessons from simple to complex. Don't make any lesson vague. -Leela
- I wish I had had at least a minimal amount of L1 (Spanish) support. Nonetheless, I now feel that having been forced into an English-only, total immersion experience was good. It motivated me to learn English fast. –Francisco
- I wouldn't change anything! -Yari
- Don't assume, ask. –AN-Bhutan
- I would want her to help me not be so shy. -Birtukan
- I would ask around about the culture, habits and the education system that my students were raised in. Then I would wean them from that style to American style in a piecemeal fashion. -Babak
- I would want her to have a translator more, or a translator tool to help me. –Karla
- I would change nothing. -Gadson
- Nothing, she was great. –AN1

Was there something in particular that made learning English easier for you? Something at school or at home?

- The language was really hard for me. It helped me that my new teacher used a lot of "sight language" to talk to me. She really used her hands and her face and her body when she was talking, so I could put everything together and then it could make sense. Also, she wrote down all of the things I would need, like my lunch number. –Samir
- Practice! Lots of practice. –AN1
- When I came back [to America] after I had forgotten all my English, TV was a great resource for me. My mom made me read and write a lot. -Yari
- Some people at my apartments spoke English. They would teach me at home or when we were playing. -Zar

- Watching English news and English movies and documentaries. -Leela
- Yes. In fact, telling us stories (mostly chapter books) would help the students visualize the word and help get the word into their smart brains. –Gadson
- Hanging out with my American friends. -Babak
- My home language in the United States was Spanish. However, at school, I was in an English-only, language-rich environment, in which teachers read to us and encouraged us to read, where I interacted with L1 English speakers in and out of the classroom, and where I felt safe. -Francisco
- Friends from same cultural backgrounds. –AN-Bhutan
- Mostly my dad. He used to translate for the U.S. when we lived in Iraq, so he already knew a lot of English. He is good at teaching us and my mom. Also, I learned a lot from watching TV and YouTube in English. –Fahad
- It was easier to learn in a smaller classroom environment. -Jor
- It helped me when someone explained things to me in my own language, like another student or a translator. I learned a lot from the computer, too. –Lamyia
- Having other kids translate was the best thing for me. Also, another student made me feel better because he showed me that actually, English and Spanish can be really alike. –Karla
- I had a friend, Rufta. She spoke my language. It was really easier having her by my side. She came about six months after me, so I knew just a little bit more English. I helped her with math. I started speaking more after I had Rufta. -Birtukan
- My first friend Amber and my mom because they were very supportive of me. –Jemima

What school activities do you think helped you the most in learning English?

- Interactive study. –Leela
- I would say drama because you got to act out the things that were said and Imagine Learning (computerized language learning) after school program. -Yari
- I think intervention groups really boosted my academic knowledge. -Jor
- Interacting with classmates helped enormously. Projects, such as making posters and presenting them, as well as skits, all contributed to accelerating my learning of English. –Francisco
- ESL coursework. –AN-Bhutan
- Playing with the kids outside. -Birtukan
- A normal routine helped me. Also, my teacher gave us all numbers and called them from sticks. Then I knew when I was supposed to talk. -Fahad
- Social activities. –Babak
- Activating background knowledge, collaboration, and hands on activities. -Elvina
- Playing and learning at the same time really helped me. -Zar
- Small groups helped me learn English. –Lamyia

- Reading groups helped me the most. – Karla
- Introducing myself to new people. –Jemima
- I learned a lot of English from the computer programs, like Imagine Learning. –Samir
- Informal gatherings, small group conversation. –AN1-Chile

**If you could give Newcomer *teachers* one piece of advice
in working with students from your country it would be:**

- I would say push the kids until they feel confident enough to push themselves. Also, try to find things associated with their culture. -Yari
- Don't pressure students too much. Try to help them learn the basics of English. – Birtukan
- Learn the culture and the language. Learn the American way when you are at school to avoid being judged inaccurately. Practice speaking aloud and make a lot of mistakes. It's okay! -Elvina
- To take an Arabic lesson and to learn how Iraq was destroyed. –Lamyia
- Try to evaluate students before you start the lesson. Plan accordingly if you have different levels of students. Please start your teaching with beginners level. -Leela
- Get a translator!! –Karla
- Listen to what I have to say. Think of me as an individual, and not part of one culture or religion. –AN-Bhutan
- Don't get too relaxed [with instruction]. –AN-Chile
- Don't assume they are rude or ungrateful unless you teach them how to act the way you want them to act. Teach them the culture, the American way before you judge them (academically and behaviorally). -Elvina
- In the case of Mexican learners, have them work with other learners (especially with non-Spanish speakers), while encouraging them to express their thoughts in English from the outset. –Francisco
- Try finding another student who knows English and a new student's [heritage] language to support fellow friends. -Jor
- They shouldn't give [Newcomers] special treatment because other students might bully them for being a teacher's pet. –Jemima
- Be caring and the rest would be easy. -Babak
- Make math fun. Then challenge the students with fun games so they could get used to having the teacher around. It is also a fun idea to take them outside so they could get used to [the new surroundings]. –Gadson
- Due to my own (sometimes painful) experiences as a 6-year-old Newcomer, I would encourage teachers to get training in dealing with ELLs. You do not have to be a bilingual teacher to develop strategies to help ELLs learn math, geography, history, or any other subject. –Francisco

If you could give first year Newcomer *students* one piece of advice it would be:

- To young Newcomers I would say: Keep your eyes and ears open. Notice what the teacher and your classmates are doing and try to use the words they use. -Francisco
- Never let what other kids say to you keep you from achieving something greater in life. –Jemima
- Be friendly and hang out with every one. We are all the same and we have a lot in common. Do not worry and do not judge a book by its cover. –Babak
- Learn the culture and the language. Learn the American way when you are at school to avoid being judged inaccurately. Practice speaking aloud and make a lot of mistakes. It's okay! -Elvina
- STOP BULLYING. –AN-Bhutan
- School in America is really good! –Lamyia
- Students should go beyond what they learn in class. Always be curious and ask lots of questions. –AN1
- English and Spanish are really alike! –Karla
- Please keep yourselves in first place as a first time student at school. -Leela
- Don't bully. And don't worry, you will be welcomed. Do not be scared to ask teachers or anybody for help. -Zar
- Please help me with more reading instead of free time. My reading isn't really great right now and I wish I read more when I was first learning English. –Obed
- To try their best to fit in. And not to worry, as long as they work hard and think smart. –Gadson
- Please don't be scared. There are teachers and students who want to help and be your friend. -Birtukan
- Don't be scared. It might be something new, but you will like it! -Yari
- Help someone else and be a translator if you can. –Fahad
- Don't worry if people are different from you; it doesn't matter. -Jor

ABOUT THE AUTHOR

Louise El Yaafouri (Kreuzer) is a consultant, author and keynote speaker in the area of refugee and immigrant ESL education. She guides districts, schools and teachers in ensuring socio-academic success for *all* learners and cultivating positive culture in diverse learning places. Areas of specialization include: counseling stakeholders in crafting and refining impactful Newcomer ESL programming, facilitating parent-school connectivity, and providing exceptional professional development experiences.

Louise has extensive experience as a Newcomer educator and teacher coach. She works closely with national, state, and local resettlement entities and is an established researchers and author on the subject. *The Newcomer Student: An Educator's Guide to Aid Transition* (Rowman & Littlefield International), Louise's first text, was published in 2016. Louise has contributed to various publications and speaks at national and international educational events.

www.ingramcontent.com/pod-product-compliance
Lightning Source LLC
Chambersburg PA
CBHW080733230426
43665CB00020B/2720